Profile for Profitability:
Using Cost Control
and Profitability Analysis

WILEY SERIES ON SYSTEMS AND CONTROLS FOR FINANCIAL MANAGEMENT

Edited by Robert L. Shultis and Frank Mastromano

EDP Systems for Credit Management
Conan D. Whiteside

Profile for Profitability: Using Cost Control and Profitability Analysis
Thomas S. Dudick

Zero-Base Budgeting
Peter A. Pyhrr

Profile for Profitability:

Using Cost Control
and Profitability Analysis

THOMAS S. DUDICK

ERNST & ERNST

A Wiley-Interscience Publication

JOHN WILEY & SONS
New York · London · Sydney · Toronto

Library of Congress Cataloging in Publication Data:

Dudick, Thomas S
  Profile for profitability.
  (Wiley series on systems and controls for financial management)
  1. Industrial management. 2. Cost control.
3. Profit. I. Title.

HD47.5.D82   658.1'55   72-4353
ISBN 0-471-22362-X

Printed in the United States of America

10-9 8 7 6 5 4 3 2 1

Dedicated to my children

JONI, STEPHEN, and KEVIN

ACKNOWLEDGMENTS

Portions of the material included in this book were taken from articles written by Thomas S. Dudick and published in *Management Adviser, Journal of Accountancy, Managerial Planning, Financial Executive, Management Accounting, and Industry Week.*

Also by Thomas S. Dudick
  Cost Controls for Industry, Prentice-Hall, 1962

SERIES PREFACE

No one needs to tell the reader that the world is changing. He sees it all too clearly. The immutable, the constant, the unchanging of a decade or two ago no longer represent the latest thinking—on *any* subject, whether morals, medicine, politics, economics, or religion. Change has always been with us, but the pace has been accelerating, especially in the postwar years.

Business, particularly with the advent of the electronic computer some 20 years ago, has also undergone change. New disciplines have sprung up. New professions are born. New skills are in demand. And the need is ever greater to blend the new skills with those of the older professions to meet the demands of modern business.

The accounting and financial functions certainly are no exception. The constancy of change is as pervasive in these fields as it is in any other. Industry is moving toward an integration of many of the information gathering, processing, and analyzing functions under the impetus of the so-called systems approach. Such corporate territory has been, traditionally, the responsibility of the accountant and the financial man. It still is, to a large extent—but times are changing.

Does this, then, spell the early demise of the accountant as we know him today? Does it augur a lessening of influence for the financial specialists in today's corporate hierarchy? We think not. We maintain, however, that it is incumbent upon today's accountant and today's financial man to learn *today's* thinking and to *use today's* skills. It is for this reason the Wiley Series on Systems and Controls for Financial Management is being developed.

Recognizing the broad spectrum of interests and activities that the series title encompasses, we plan a number of volumes, each representing the latest thinking, written by a recognized authority, on a particular facet of the financial man's responsibilities. The subjects contemplated for discussion within the series range from production accounting systems to planning, to corporate records, to control of cash. Each book is an in-depth study of one subject within this group. Each is intended to be a practical, working tool for the businessman in general and the financial man and accountant in particular.

Robert L. Shultis

Frank M. Mastromano

PREFACE

This is a book on profitability. It provides the reader with a better insight into answers to such questions as: How profitable should my business be? What are the areas of weakness? and How can I improve profits?

It is a broad review of the various aspects of profitability rather than a narrow treatment slanted toward financial management.

Why This Book Is Needed

By reading the illustrations representing other company experiences, the reader will obtain an overview through which he will see his own company in a different perspective. This difference in vantage point will not provide an "instant" solution, but it will raise questions, the answers to which can be most revealing.

This is not a textbook dissertation on the theory of profits, but a discussion using "real-life" examples of how the profitability of a business can be enhanced.

How This Book Is Developed

In Section I, a "how-to" illustration shows how to analyze a troubled company's financial position. Another case study demonstrates how a group of executives can diagnose weaknesses within their company for the purpose of coming up with corrective action.

Section II goes on to explain what steps must be taken to assure that operations will be profitable—covering such topics as the importance of looking at the big picture, how profits can be improved through proper use of cost measurement techniques, and the importance of effective utilization of equipment. One of the cases illustrates how a company evaluated its product profitability, starting with an uncertain sales forecast and winding up with important cost savings ideas. Another case demonstrates, for nonstandard products and services, how profitable operations can be assured. It starts with the classification of expenses, the reporting, and control by element, tieing the actual costs back to the original estimate on which the price was based, and it demonstrates how profit projections are made into future periods.

This section also discusses the importance of, and describes the steps required for, properly evaluating the profitability of a new venture.

Section III concerns itself with feedback as to what results have been achieved and the reasons profits have deviated from what they had been anticipated to be. It discusses how professional managers are under pressure because of demanding stockholders and it makes a five-point recommendation for improving profits. The important subjects of cost flow, effect of inventory valuation on reported profits, and use of various statement formats are also covered in this section.

Highlights of the Book

The book covers a range of problems facing the executive whose effectiveness is measured by the profitability of his operation. The reader who is interested in improving the profits of his business will find out how:

· Productive capacity can be increased without heavy commitments in fixed facilities.
· The first-line supervisor can reduce costs five ways.
· An automobile parts distributor, through a systematic financial analysis put his finger on the three major trouble spots that led to decisions which took him out of trouble and made his operations profitable.
· A professional manager pressed by his stockholders for profits reduced costs.
· A group of key management executives, through a systematic

comparison of the results of their company with the industry averages, spotted a number of trouble spots in their company—the correction of which upped profits by 50% in one year with no increase in volume.

· A flexible budget can be a dynamic management tool for making important cost reductions *before* finalization rather than after.

· The HiFi-Stereo Corporation, by focusing on the big picture, came up with a number of cost reduction ideas that helped it to exceed its profit goals.

· A company that wanted to become big stunted its profits by expanding too fast. By a careful evaluation of the problems it had experienced in the past, it adopted a set of ten commandments for expansion. Profits came to life and at the end of three years the company tripled its previous rate of return.

Competitive pressures are the greatest they have ever been in the history of our country—and they are becoming increasingly greater. The effect of competition on profits is only too well known. This is the reason professional managers must stand back and reappraise every facet of their businesses. This book is intended to help accomplish this.

THOMAS S. DUDICK

Middletown, New Jersey
June 1972

CONTENTS

Activities within a business are linked to external economic forces. Once a relationship with these forces is established, business goals can be tied to logical reference points.

Financial ratios are indicators that can be used in comparing one company's financial position with that of another—and with the industry average. The troubles of an automotive parts distributor are diagnosed.

The true makeup of productivity indicators is frequently obscured because broad measures are generally used. These assume that cost reductions are based entirely on improved methods. This chapter illustrates three such indicators and it also describes a recommended approach which is more actionable than the broad type. The figures used for demonstrating this method point up that all conversion costs, not only fixed overhead, are affected by changes in volume.

Many medium-sized companies, too large for direct face-to-face communication, too small for elaborate information systems, can benefit enormously from well-planned, well-guided management meetings. Such meetings can do much to ferret out serious trouble spots for corrective action.

When sound business policies are subordinated to rapid growth, profits suffer and liquidation of past gains is the inevitable result. This chapter describes a pattern that has been typical for many companies, and it recommends a set of guidelines for orderly growth in the form of "ten commandments for expansion."

SECTION II   ASSURING PROFITABLE OPERATIONS

A well thought-out profit plan allows management to evaluate the various probabilities and alternatives in advance. Then, when things go "off course," management will already have had its "fire drills" and will be far better equipped to cope with the unforeseen.

Plans for the new year are frequently impeded because of delays in forecasting sales. This chapter explains how flexible budget techniques can be employed in minimizing the effect of such delays. It also emphasizes that formalization of a flexible budget can be a highly informative tool to key executives-leading to important cost savings.

Unlike earlier case studies, this one, for a job costing operation, covers a broad spectrum. It starts with classification of expenses, reporting, and control by element of cost, relating these elements back to the estimate used to develop the price, and goes on to cash forecasting and profit projection. This chapter is "must" reading for anyone doing work for the government.

9   A Commonsense Approach to Profit Improvement   125

Cost control methods applied to raw materials and direct labor can work well only if the men on the line—the supervisors—are aware of costs and the relative efficiency of their operations.

10   Evaluating Profit Opportunities in a New Business Venture   138

Assuring profitable operations in a going business frequently requires only modification of existing procedures. A new venture, however, must be evaluated from ground up—there are no existing procedures to modify.

11   Utilization of Investment and its Relation to Profitability   161

The key to profitability is the effective utilization of investment. Good control of inventories and efficient utilization of facilities contributes far more to profitability than comparing dollars spent with dollars budgeted.

12   The Economy and Its Effect on Profitability   177

The impact that the state of the economy can have on profits is well known. Herein lies the clue as to whether modern business should make its plans based on one set of assumptions or whether plans should be formulated through a recognition of the range of possibilities based on both an optimistic and a pessimistic look at the future.

SECTION III   IMPORTANCE OF MEANINGFUL FEEDBACK

13   Pressures on the Professional Manager for Profits   183

The professional manager of a publicly owned company is subjected not only to the normal competitive pressures of the marketplace—he is also pressured by the stockholder who demands an optimum return on his investment even though he may have unwisely purchased his stock at too high a price. This chapter reviews some of the steps that can be taken to improve return on investment.

14   Getting Behind the Operating Statement   190

It is not enough to look at the overall figures on profitability. The perceptive manager who is not financially oriented needs a better insight into cost flow, as well as a knowledge of the profitability of his products by class of sale.

15   Which Statement Format Shall I Look At?   206

A proliferation of statement formats can be confusing and annoying to the busy executive who must have facts on which to base decisions. This chapter discusses four basic formats and demonstrates the use and application of each.

16   Explaining Deviations from Planned Profits   218

The analysis of variances in some companies has become a fine art in the practice of mathematics without really throwing much light on the problem. When the approach is formula-oriented, the amount and type of variance can vary depending upon which formula is used.

17   Alternative Costing Methods   231

Executives who must run their businesses profitably are confused by the diversity of opinion among their professional advisers. Do such executives care whether the cost system is called "direct" or "absorption," or are they primarily interested in results?

18 Summing Up   240

If the three sections of this book were to be labeled with single word descriptions, these three words would be: measurement, efficiency, and feedback. Accordingly, this chapter recaps the indicators used for measurement, stresses the need for efficient operations and discusses the importance of correcting common defects in providing information to management.

SECTION I

Indicators of Profitability

CHAPTER 1

USE OF INDICATORS

Activities within a business are linked to external economic forces. Once a relationship with these forces is established, business goals can be tied to logical reference points.

Planning for profits is an important management responsibility which often is not followed with the degree of diligence that such responsibility warrants. An important tool for planning profits is the indicator: an index that serves to relate various aspects of a business to external economic forces.

Indicators used in business are not as precise as road maps are to the driver of a car. They are more like a compass—pointing to the general direction from which more detailed judgments must be made. To achieve maximum precision consistent with economy of application, the indicator selected should be the one that best relates the activity to be measured with the external force to which it relates.

Population growth, for example, is a generally accepted indicator for projecting volume of construction. However, in planning for certain segments of government—school construction, for example—a more precise indicator is required. In this instance population statistics by age group and density are used. If the plan is to build a given number of classrooms for elementary, junior high, and high school grades, population growth by age group provides a far more precise indicator against which to plan than total population statistics. The same principle applies to business with equal force. If an existing indicator is not sufficiently representative of activity because it is too broad, then refinements must be introduced.

Sometimes no indicator is available. In such a circumstance it may be necessary to find a relationship with some other available indicator. An illustration of one such case is a company producing a new type of dairy product. The company wanted to establish controls to monitor its penetration to the potential market.

Since detailed national statistics for dairy products were not available in the breakdown needed, the management of this company made a careful study to determine whether its product could be tied to total food statistics which were available in the desired breakdown. The study showed a very close correlation. Therefore, in determining its planned share of the market areas, total food statistics were used as a guide. Thereafter, actual sales of this company's products were compared with the figures for the food industry to arrive at guides for management as to progress in achieving its goals in increasing its share of the market in various areas of the country.

MAJOR AND MINOR INDICATORS

Indicators vary in importance depending upon the individual using them. The president of a company and the stockholders, for example, in stating their expectations for the coming year, frequently express their goals in terms of so many dollars profit per share of stock, or a certain percentage return on investment. These are major indicators to this level of management.

To the sales manager and the manufacturing manager, these do not represent major indicators. The sales manager is more concerned with the dollar sales volume by product line required to meet such a goal. The manufacturing manager is more concerned with such factors as production efficiency, utilization of equipment, and amount of scrap or rework. The methods engineer is interested in the number of set-ups and changeovers, while in the personnel department a more meaningful measure is the number of employees in the various classifications to be hired so that production volume goals can be achieved. The quality control manager is the least of all interested directly in the return on investment goals since his mission is to maintain a high quality level.

In short, even though every level of management may strive toward achieving the same end goal, the indicators for each level must necessarily be different. What is a major indicator for one segment of management is undoubtedly of minor significance to others.

NUMERICAL VERSUS NARRATIVE INDICATORS

Progress against goals in some endeavors cannot always be expressed conveniently by an all-encompassing numerical indicator. A good example is the space program which started in 1957 when the Russians launched Sputnik. As a result of public clamor to surpass Russia's space feats, substantial sums of money were appropriated to the National Aeronautical and Space Administration to launch a gigantic space effort. This required the establishment of centers such as the Houston and Kennedy space centers. Worldwide tracking stations had to be built, launching pads constructed, and various types of vehicles developed and built. Also of importance was the establishment of public relations to keep the public informed. The progress on this program could hardly be monitored through a numerical indicator. Since the goal was to surpass Russia by sending a man to the moon first, this was the target or plan. Since no numerical indicator could possibly keep the public apprised of progress, it was necessary to do this in narrative fashion. So, in effect, the complete story from plan to achievements to date was told in the following manner. "Our plan is to place a man on the moon by 1970. Here's where we stand against that plan. . . ."

Research and development projects in the business community are another example of how numerical indicators are not always an appropriate yardstick. The progress of an engineer on a research project is hard to evaluate and express in terms of a statistic. For that reason, as in the case of the space program, a verbal or narrative type of indicator relates the goal to be achieved, what has been achieved to date, how far away the goal might be, what problems are being encountered, and possibly revised estimates of target accomplishment dates. This does not, however, rule out the use of numerical data to support a verbal or narrative indicator.

DOLLARS ARE NOT ALWAYS THE MOST SIGNIFICANT DENOMINATOR

Just as numerical data do not always fulfill the requirements of a good indicator, so does the use of dollars in certain instances fall short of presenting the facts in the most meaningful manner. Although certain types of financial data can never be reported in other than dollar denominators, the underlying information making up the dollars is often much more actionable if reported in units. Number of employees, units of product, labor hours, machine hours, months of inventory, or number of days' receivables are some examples.

Number of Employees versus Payroll

The United States military organization is probably the best illustration of the importance of reporting men as opposed to dollars of payroll. Each military installation must each day report its strength by grade and by duty status, that is, in confinement, in hospital, on leave, AWOL, or missing. This information is consolidated for an entire base, and then forwarded to a higher level for further consolidation with information from other bases. This provides day-by-day information on the total strength of the services. These figures are then continually related to planned tables of organization and used as a basis for calling up more men. The strength by grade and by duty is further analyzed by MOS (military occupational specialty) to compare the actual number of incumbents in each grade and MOS with the planned requirements. With this type of information decisions as to size and availability of reserves can be made.

In business, as in the military organization, accountability by number of employees in the various segments of management is an important control figure. In many businesses payrolls account for approximately two-thirds to three-quarters of the total indirect costs of operating the business. While knowledge of the total payroll cost in dollars is an essential figure to have, it does not provide management with a sufficiently actionable figure in terms of dollars, except on a broad basis.

One company faced with a quickly deteriorating profit picture found it helpful to receive a manning report on a week-to-week basis. It had consolidated two operations under one roof for purposes of cost reduction. Accordingly, a personnel reduction goal was established in each department of the company. The number of employees on the payroll in each of these departments was reported weekly, with the preceding weeks' figures reproduced so that progress over the weeks could be readily monitored.

The report is shown in Table 1-1.

A report such as that shown in Table 1-1 quickly highlights progress against the plan. While emphasis is given to number of workers rather than to payroll dollars, it is not always desirable to limit reporting to number of employees alone. Let us use the maintenance department as a case in point. Although the number of men had been reduced from 36 to 27 with a good possibility that the goal of 24 men would be attained by the target date, the overtime dollars showed a different trend. For the weeks included in Table 1-1, the payments were:

2/16	$492
2/23	480
3/1	478
3/8	510
3/15	533
3/22	629
3/29	617
4/5	605
4/12	595
4/19	653
4/26	618
5/3	626
5/10	737
Target 5/31	250

The overtime, which at 2/16 had been about double the target of $250 per week, was at 5/10 almost three times as great as the plan. While this might raise the question as to whether the cuts in personnel were made too deeply, investigation revealed that an unusual

Table 1-1 Breakdown of Indirect Employees

Week Ending	General Manager's Office	Mainten- ance	Manufac- turing Adminis- tration	Production Control	Pur- chasing	Quality Control	Total
2/16	7	36	50	128	46	20	287
2/23	7	36	49	126	45	19	282
3/1	7	36	49	125	43	19	279
3/8	7	33	48	118	42	19	267
3/15	7	32	46	116	41	18	260
3/22	6	29	40	116	39	18	248
3/29	6	29	39	116	38	18	246
4/5	6	29	39	113	38	18	243
4/12	6	28	38	112	38	18	240
4/19	6	28	38	111	37	18	238
4/26	5	28	37	110	37	18	235
5/3	5	28	36	108	36	17	230
5/10	5	27	35	108	35	17	227
5/17							
5/24							
Target for 5/31	5	24	28	98	35	16	206

amount of overhauling of equipment was being performed during that period in order to catch up with long neglected maintenance.

Further cuts in maintenance personnel were suspended until the overhaul program was finished—in order to avoid the extra cost of premium payments for overtime. This study also pointed out to management that certain types of equipment being overhauled were being superseded in the market by more advanced equipment. In such instances older and slower machines were scrapped rather than rebuilt. Staffing of the maintenance department was adjusted accordingly.

UTILIZATION OF EQUIPMENT

As our technology advances and the use of high cost automated equipment increases, the degree to which such equipment is utilized becomes more and more important. The percentage of available hours that machines are productively employed becomes an important indicator which must be communicated to the department head responsible for profitable operation of the equipment.

Airlines recognize the dynamic nature of utilization because they have determined that a jet plane loses $3000 in revenue for every hour that it is idle. Also, the breakeven point becomes a very important indicator. One overseas airline finds that its breakeven point is represented by approximately 40% seat occupancy. Another airline, which is entirely domestic and therefore has shorter runs, finds that its breakeven point is closer to 55%.

And so it is in the other segments of industry where investment in equipment is high. Management must be well informed as to what its breakeven point is so its planned or desired level of operations can be established. Then, through regular reports, the actual level is compared with the planned level, and deviations communicated to management for appropriate action.

ANALYSIS OF INDICATORS THROUGH GRAPHIC PRESENTATION

Since the purpose of using an indicator is to provide a basis for comparing actual happenings with an indicator that is representative, graphs can frequently be employed to advantage.

Exhibit 1-1

COMPARISON OF SALES, NET INCOME
AND SHARE OF MARKET

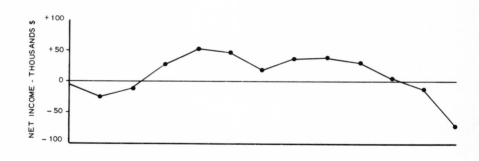

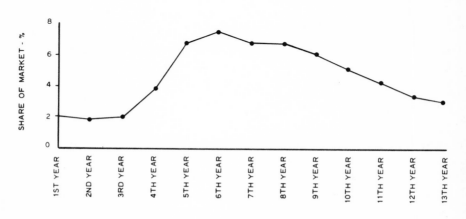

Consider Exhibit 1-1, for example. Although the figures for sales and net income are disguised, the trends are accurately depicted and the share of market is correctly shown. The key item is net income, which is compared with two indicators: sales and share of market.

Past history indicates that this company loses money when its share of market begins to approach a 3% level. The 3% does not always represent the same dollar volume of sales, however. Note, for example, that between the third and fourth years, 3% is represented by a sales volume slightly in excess of $400,000, while between the twelfth and thirteenth years, a 3% share is closer to $800,000.

This observation may be somewhat surprising to those who attempt to develop breakeven analyses for the long term through use of a mathematical formula developed from short range projections.

This chapter has pointed out the importance of linking the activities within a business with some external economic force which will act as a bellwether. Once the relationship with the most appropriate indicators has been established, the business will have the assurance that planning is tied to a logical reference point.

In addition, this chapter has highlighted the value of various statistical indicators which are often as important to management, if not more so, as the conventional accounting reports. Accountants would do well to utilize the available indicators in their periodic communications with management.

CHAPTER 2

DIAGNOSING A BUSINESS THROUGH USE OF FINANCIAL INDICATORS

Financial ratios are indicators that can be used in comparing one company's financial position with that of another—and with the industry average. The troubles of an automotive parts distributor are diagnosed.

The effective professional manager or owner of a business recognizes the importance of being able to analyze business activities through all available techniques, and leaves no stone unturned in his efforts to become more intimately familiar with his business. Financial ratios provide one such technique. Although this type ratio tends to be more subjective than the types of indicators discussed earlier, they do utilize a link outside the particular company through a comparison with similar financial ratios for the industry. A discussion of the makeup and use of such ratios is given in this chapter.

WHAT ARE FINANCIAL RATIOS?

Financial ratios may be defined as diagnostic indicators of the health of a business. Of the 2½ to 3 million businesses in existence in the United States, many fail each year and are replaced by new ones. Reasons for failure include such practices as undisciplined expansion, overextension of credit to customers, and overinvestment in inventory and in facilities.

An example of how a financial ratio can be informative to management can be demonstrated by the number of days of outstanding receivables. While sales volume may be highly pleasing to the volume-minded "order taker," a look at the average collection period may reveal that the collection period exceeds the terms of sale beyond a safety factor. In addition to tying up the company's cash, the poor collection ratio often leads to uncollectible accounts which must be written off.

Relating inventories to sales (or cost of sales) is another indicator of possible trouble when the ratio shows a higher-than-industry ratio. Not only is excessive capital tied up when the ratio is unfavorable—the risk of obsolescence increases.

Financial ratios provide management with danger signals to warn of impending trouble. Customarily, these figures are compared with the composite ratio for industry in general (as well as with its own past experience), to determine out-of-line situations. Dun & Bradstreet, in its annual publication, "Key Business Ratios," lists 14 such indicators. They are:

Current Assets to Current Debt

Current assets are divided by total current debt to obtain this ratio. Current assets are the sum of cash, notes, and accounts receivable (less reserves for bad debt), advances on merchandise, merchandise inventories, and listed, federal, state, and municipal securities not in excess of market value. Current debt is the total of all liabilities falling due within one year. This is one test of solvency.

Net Profits on Net Sales

This figure is obtained by dividing the net earnings of the business, after taxes, by net sales (the dollar volume less returns, allowances, and cash discounts).

Net Profits on Tangible Net Worth

Tangible net worth is the equity of stockholders in the business, as obtained by subtracting total liabilities from total assets and then deducting intangibles. The ratio is obtained by dividing net profits after taxes by tangible net worth. The tendency is to look increasingly to this ratio as a final criterion of profitability. Generally, a relationship of at least 10% is regarded as a desirable objective for providing dividends plus funds for future growth.

Net Profits on Net Working Capital

Net working capital represents the excess of current assets over current debt. This margin represents the cushion available to the business for carrying inventories and receivables and for financing day-to-day operations. The ratio is obtained by dividing net profits, after taxes, by net working capital.

Net Sales to Tangible Net Worth

Net sales are divided by tangible net worth to obtain this figure. This gives a measure of relative turnover of invested capital.

Net Sales to Net Working Capital

Net sales are divided by net working capital to obtain this figure. This provides a guide as to the extent the company is turning its working capital and the margin of operating funds.

Collection Period

Annual net sales are divided by 365 days to obtain average daily credit sales, and then the average daily credit sales are divided into notes and accounts receivable, including any that have been discounted. This ratio is helpful in analyzing the collectibility of receivables. Many observers feel the collection period should not exceed the net maturity indicated by selling terms by more than 10 to

15 days. When comparing the collection period of one concern with that of another, allowances should be made for possible variations in selling terms.

Net Sales to Inventory

Dividing annual net sales by merchandise inventory as carried on the balance sheet results in this figure. This quotient does not yield an actual physical turnover. It provides a yardstick for comparing stock-to-sales ratios of one concern with those of another or with those for the industry.

Fixed Assets to Tangible Net Worth

Fixed assets are divided by tangible net worth to obtain this figure. Fixed assets represent depreciated book values of buildings, leasehold improvements, machinery, furniture, fixtures, tools, and other physical equipment, plus land, if any, valued at cost or appraised market value. Ordinarily, this relationship should not exceed 100% for a manufacturer and 75% for a wholesaler or retailer.

Current Debt to Tangible Net Worth

This figure is derived by dividing current debt by tangible net worth. Ordinarily, a business is in trouble when this relationship exceeds 80%.

Total Debt to Tangible Net Worth

This figure is obtained by dividing total current debts plus long term debts by tangible net worth. When this relationship exceeds 100%, the equity of creditors in the assets of the business exceeds that of the owners.

Inventory to Net Working Capital

Merchandise inventory is divided by net working capital to obtain this figure. This is an additional measure of inventory balance. Ordinarily, the relationship should not exceed 80%.

Current Debt to Inventory

Dividing the current debt by inventory yields yet another indication of the extent to which the business relies on funds from disposal of unsold inventories to meet its debts.

Funded Debt to Net Working Capital

Funded debts are all long term obligations, as represented by mortgages, bonds, debentures, term loans, serial notes, and other types of liabilities maturing more than one year from the statement date. This ratio is obtained by dividing funded debt by net working capital. Analysts tend to compare funded debt with net working capital in determining whether or not long term debts are in proper proportion. Ordinarily, this relationship should not exceed 100%.

These 14 ratios are arranged on a worksheet (Exhibit 2-1) in a form that facilitates the computation of the individual ratios. Use of such a form is particularly convenient when comparisons are being made for several years. Watching the year-by-year trend within a company is as important as making comparisons with the industry average.

To illustrate how this worksheet can be used in making a financial analysis for Automotive Rebuilders, Inc., a statement of income and a balance sheet are shown as Exhibits 2-2 and 2-3. The pertinent items contained in these statements are interpreted into financial ratios in Exhibit 2-4.

HOW THE FINANCIAL RATIO WORKSHEET IS USED

In demonstrating the use of the worksheet referred to as Exhibit 2-1, it is not necessary to explain in detail the calculation of all 14 ratios.

Exhibit 2-1 Financial Ratio Worksheet

	Current Assets to Current Liabilities (Times)	Net Profit on Net Sales (%)	Net Profits on Tangible Net Worth (%)	Net Profits on Net Working Capital (%)	Net Sales to Tangible Net Worth (Times)	Net Sales to Net Working Capital (Times)	Collection Period (Days)

	Net Sales to Inventory (Times)	Fixed Assets to Tangible Net Worth (%)	Current Liability to Tangible Net Worth (%)	Total Liability to Tangible Net Worth (%)	Inventory to Net Working Capital (%)	Current Liabilities to Inventory (%)	Cost of Goods Sold to Sales (%)

Exhibit 2-2 Automotive Rebuilders, Inc. Statement of Income for Current Year

Sales		$189,375.54
Cost of sales		
Materials	$45,687.81	
Payroll	75,673.79	
Cost of sales		121,361.60
Gross Profit on sales		$ 68,013.94
Expenses		
Officers' salaries	$13,000.00	
Office and drivers' salaries	19,170.00	
Payroll taxes	5,709.12	
Employee benefits	549.59	
Rent	7,640.00	
Light and power	2,767.45	
Telephone	985.96	
Shop expenses and supplies	5,263.40	
Advertising and commissions	1,727.68	
Insurance	1,580.34	
Interest	3,120.06	
Automobile expense	2,383.96	
Other expenses	2,047.06	
Total expenses		65,944.62
Net profits before depreciation and bad debts		$ 2,069.32
Less depreciation and bad debts		
Depreciation	$ 2,185.16	
Bad debts	3,080.94	
Total depreciation and bad debts		$ 5,266.10
Net loss for the year		$ 3,196.78

Since balance sheet figures are used in some of the ratios, income statement figures in others, and a combination of the two for the third group, it might be well to use illustrative examples for each of the three:

Current Ratio

This is the first of the 14 ratios shown on the worksheet. Since this ratio is determined by dividing the current assets by the current liabilities, the current assets are recorded in Exhibit 2-4 as the numerator, while the current liabilities are shown as the denominator. By dividing the numerator $45,895 by the denominator $30,586, we find that the current ratio is 1.50, which means that the company has $1.50 of such current assets as cash, money owed by customers and inventory for every dollar of current liabilities, represented by money owed to suppliers, notes payable to banks, and accrued expenses such as payroll.

By comparing this current ratio of 1.50 with the industry average of 2.83, it is obvious that the company's working capital is impaired because it does not have as many dollars of current assets to cover current debts as its competitors have. Comparing the current ratio with the company's ratio for prior years shows whether there has been an improvement or regression.

Net Profit on Net Sales

This is a commonly used ratio whereby profits are shown as the numerator and net sales as the denominator. In two of these years, net profits are actually losses so the calculation of a ratio in such instances is academic. Here, as in the current ratio, it is evident that the company does not compare favorably with the industry.

Collection Period

This ratio is somewhat more complex than the others because it must be computed in two steps:

Exhibit 2-3 Automotive Rebuilders, Inc. Balance Sheet for Current Year

Current assets			
Cash in bank		$ 153.48	
Accounts receivable	$31,152.90		
Less due to factor	13,461.37	17,691.53	
Merchandise			
inventory		28,050.50	
Total current assets			$45,895.51

Fixed assets	Cost	Accumulated depreciation	Net book value	
Machinery and				
equipment	$ 5,175.84	$ 4,003.57	$ 1,172.27	
Furniture and				
fixtures	2,073.89	1,145.83	928.06	
Autos and trucks	5,787.00	3,310.26	2,476.74	
Improvements	1,100.00	660.00	440.00	
Total fixed assets	$14,136.73	$ 9,119.66		5,017.07

Other assets			
Deposits as security		$ 1,800.00	
Loans to employees		115.00	
Total other assets			1,915.00
Total assets			$52,827.58

1. The year's sales, as the numerator, are divided by 365 days to determine the sales per day.

$$\frac{\$189,376 \text{ (sales)}}{365 \text{ (days)}} = \$518 \text{ (sales per day)}$$

2. The accounts receivable $31,153, as the numerator, is then divided by the sales per day to arrive at the number of days' receivables that are outstanding.

$$\frac{\$31,153 \text{ (accounts receivable)}}{\$518 \text{ (sales per day)}} = 60 \text{ (days' receivables outstanding)}$$

Here again, the company does not show up favorably with the in-

Exhibit 2-3 (Continued)

Liabilities and capital			
Current liabilities			
Accounts payable		$23,131.69	
Notes payable, Bank		1,032.90	
Notes payable, General Motors Acceptance Corporation		843.30	
Payroll and expenses accrued		5,578.12	
Total current liabilities			$30,586.01
Long term liabilities			$ 4,546.41
Capital			
Capital stock		$20,000.00	
Retained earnings, last year	$ 891.94		
Net loss for year	3,196.78		
Retained earnings, this year		(2,304.84)	
Total capital			$17,695.16
Total liabilities and capital			$52,827.58

dustry average—which indicates 42 days as compared with 60 days for the company.

MAKING THE ANALYSIS

It is not always necessary to go through the formality of calculating all 14 financial ratios to find trouble spots in a business. For Automotive Rebuilders, Inc. for example, the analysis reveals trends that are obvious without actually converting all the information into ratios:

1. Sales dollars have eroded badly over the three-year period, having dropped from $303,657 in the earliest year to $189,376 in the current period, more than a one-third drop.

2. The industry return of profits on sales indicates that competitors are making profits while Automotive Rebuilders is losing money.

Exhibit 2-4 Automotive Rebuilders, Inc. Financial Ratio Worksheet

	Current Assets to Current Liabilities	Net Profit on Net Sales	Net Profits on Tangible Net Worth	Net Profits on Net Working Capital	Net Sales to Tangible Net Worth	Net Sales to Net Working Capital	Collection Period[a]
	(Times)	(%)	(%)	(%)	(Times)	(Times)	(Days)
Numerator							
Current year	45,895	(3,197)	(3,197)	(3,197)	189,376	189,376	189,376
Last year	48,464	1,153	1,153	1,153	225,874	225,874	225,874
Previous year	58,898	(1,081)	(1,081)	(1,081)	303,657	303,657	303,657
Denominator							
Current year	30,586	189,376	17,695	15,309	17,695	15,309	365
Last year	28,100	225,874	22,245	20,364	22,245	20,364	365
Previous year	46,666	303,657	21,844	13,232	21,844	12,232	365
Ratios							
Current year	1.50	(1.68)	(18.06)	(20.80)	10.70	12.37	518
Last year	1.72	0.51	5.18	5.66	10.15	11.09	619
Previous year	1.26	(0.35)	(4.94)	(8.83)	13.90	24.82	832
Industry average	2.83	3.66	9.27	16.04	2.70	4.40	42

Exhibit 2-4 (Continued)

	Net Sales to Inventory	Fixed Assets to Tangible Net Worth	Current Liability to Tangible Net Worth	Total Liability to Tangible Net Worth	Inventory to Net Working Capital	Current Liabilities to Inventory	Cost of Goods Sold to Sales
	(Times)	(%)	(%)	(%)	(%)	(%)	(%)
Numerator							
Current year	189,376	5,017	30,586	35,132	28,051	30,586	121,362
Last year	225,874	6,527	48,464	32,747	21,796	28,100	152,020
Previous year	303,657	7,856	58,898	46,711	21,804	46,666	210,569
Denominator							
Current year	28,051	17,695	17,695	17,695	15,309	28,051	189,376
Last year	21,796	22,245	22,245	22,245	20,364	21,796	225,874
Previous year	21,804	21,844	21,844	21,844	12,232	21,804	303,657
Ratios							
Current year	6.8	28.4	173	199	183	109	64.1
Last year	10.4	29.3	218	147	107	129	70.0
Previous year	13.9	36.0	270	214	178	214	70.0
Industry average	5.3	37.2	33	50	75	78	75

[a] Calculation of collection period: total sales divided by number of days to arrive at sales per day; total accounts receivable then divided by sales per day.

3. Although sales in the latest year have dropped one-third, inventories over the three-year period have risen from $21,804 to $28,051—a 28% increase.

In capsule form, the trouble spots in this company can be summarized as follows:

1. Serious downward trend in sales. This company sells rebuilt generators and carburetors to wholesalers, who in turn sell to retailers. Sales are down because the manufacturers of new generators and carburetors are selling their products directly to retailers through department store outlets that feature automotive centers. In light of this the company must alter its marketing policy if it is to remain in business. It should move in the direction of selling directly to a retail-type outlet. It might establish its own automotive center and thus increase the price it receives for its products.

2. Collection policies must be tightened up to reduce the number of days now required to collect money.

3. The company must also reduce its inventories. This action, along with improvement of collections, will improve the current ratio by permitting the company to pay off its current liabilities. This in turn will result in a better debt to net worth ratio, which now shows that this company owes twice as much to creditors as its own stake in the business. Competitors, however, owe to creditors half as much as the amount of their net worth. (See Exhibit 2-4: current year's ratio of total liabilities to tangible net worth—199% is compared with the industry average of 50%.)

LIMITATIONS OF FINANCIAL RATIOS

A financial ratio, as any mathematical formula, has its limitations. When comparing one's own company with industry averages, recognition must be given to differences in valuation of inventories and variations in the methods followed in depreciating equipment.

While trade associations encourage their members to adopt uniform systems of accounting—and great strides have been made—differences still exist. Companies that have become divisions of conglomerates, for example, are required to comply with uniform accounting practices within the corporate structure. These may not always conform with practices set up for the industry.

ADVANTAGES OF USING FINANCIAL RATIOS

Although differences in practices result in variations, this may not always be indicative of weaknesses. The user of financial ratios should be aware of possible differences that might introduce bias in the comparison he is making. However, the existence of such bias is not sufficient reason for discontinuing his probing analysis into what competitors are doing. He should also be alert to differences that occur because of size, geographic area in which competitors are located, and differences in the mix of products being produced.

By persistently pursuing a policy of probing analysis and an inquisitive approach, the company can gain an excellent insight into its own weaknesses and weaknesses that exist in the industry. Proper use of operating ratios can result in improved efficiency, lower costs, and greater profits.

This type of critical analysis may not always provide the answers to questions that arise—what is important is that questions are raised. The seeking out of answers is an important avenue of investigation that leads to correction of weakness and improvement of profits.

CHAPTER 3

INDICATORS OF PRODUCTIVITY

The true makeup of productivity indicators is frequently obscured because broad measures are generally used. These assume that cost reductions are based entirely on improved methods. This chapter illustrates three such indicators and it also describes a recommended approach which is more actionable than the broad type. The figures used for demonstrating this method point up that all conversion costs, not only fixed overhead, are affected by changes in volume.

Productivity, stated simply, is the interrelationship between input and output. When output increases faster than input, there is a productivity gain. When output decreases, in terms of input, there is a productivity loss.

The introduction of automation generally means large increases in productivity. Greater productivity means more goods to be shared and therefore a higher standard of living. In backward nations the standard of living is lower than in a modern industrialized society because productivity gains, if any, are very low.

NATIONAL PRODUCTIVITY

Productivity can be measured for an entire nation or it can be identified for segments of the economy. As in any type of statistical measure, there are intangibles that defy expression in terms of a statistic. Although the productivity improvement of a nation can be expressed as, say, 3% in a particular year, it is quite difficult to assess the effect on this figure of losses due to increasing crime, exploding welfare rolls, destruction of resources during wars, additional costs to eliminate pollution, and the higher cost of more and more government services.

Measurement becomes more definitive as smaller segments of the economy are evaluated, because the effect of intangibles is usually not considered. Manufacturing is a good illustration of this.

PRODUCTIVITY IN MANUFACTURING

Productivity gains in manufacturing are not limited to the direct labor and automation aspects of manufacturing. Material, which can account for more than two-thirds of the total cost of a product, provides a potential for cost decreases. The use of sonics or lasers for cutting material, for example, can reduce losses characteristic of more conventional methods for cutting. More efficient use of material, the use of lower cost material, and better buying are some of the other practices that can result in lower unit costs for material.

Increased productivity of labor through automation sometimes results in higher unit costs for material because of the requirement for tighter material specifications.

Indirect or overhead labor can also become more productive. An illustration is the introduction of an automatic sweeping machine to replace a crew of indirect labor employees sweeping by hand. Another is the use of an automatic elevator rather than one operated manually.

MEASURING PRODUCTIVITY

There are different methods that can be employed in the measurement of productivity. Some of these are simple and quite appropriate for simpler situations.

Four different types are discussed. The choice of the one that is most appropriate for a particular activity—whether it be service or manufacturing—must be a matter of judgment as to what method fits best. Those covered are:

1. Sales basis
2. Units of output

3. Weighted units
4. Productivity trend control

Sales Basis

This is a broad measure which uses adjusted sales as the measure of output. The sales dollars for each period (annual periods assumed in the example) are reduced by the price index to adjust to constant dollars.

These adjusted sales, in terms of constant dollars, are then divided by the total man-hours in each period so that sales output per man-hour can be compared from period to period. The figures for four time periods are shown in Table 3-1.

Table 3-1   Sales Output Per Man-hour

	Period 1	Period 2	Period 3	Period 4
Sales	$100,000	$102,500	$105,000	$120,000
Price index	100.0%	100.5%	101.9%	106.9%
Sales adjusted to constant dollars	$100,000	$102,000	$103,000	$113,300
Man-hours	5,200	5,200	5,150	5,500
Sales output per man-hour	$19.23	$19.61	$20.00	$20.60
Percent change in productivity		+2.0	+1.9%	+3.0%

This method provides a measure of productivity for a company having fairly homogeneous products in its line and a relatively constant mix. The next method illustrated deals with output in units rather than in sales dollars.

Units of Output

Units of output, when available, are preferable to sales because the inaccuracies due to application of a broad price index are eliminated. The units of output method is demonstrated in Table 3-2.

Table 3-2 Units Per Man-hour

	Period 1	Period 2	Period 3	Period 4
Units produced	2400	2450	2500	2750
Man-hours	5200	5200	5150	5500
Units per man-hour	0.462	0.471	0.485	0.500
Percent change in productivity		+1.9%	+2.1%	+3.1%

While this method eliminates possible distortions due to the application of a broad-based price index, it still assumes, as did the previous example, that the units are fairly homogeneous.

The next method provides the means for equating for product differences.

Weighted Units

This method gives effect to the differences in products by using the standard man-hours required to produce each type. Each period's output is weighted by multiplying the production of each type by the man-hours required to produce it. Table 3-3 demonstrates the overall results.

Table 3-3 Weighted Manhours Per Unit

	Period 1	Period 2	Period 3	Period 4
Weighted man-hours per unit	1.980	1.945	1.907	1.851
Percent change in productivity		+1.7%	+1.9	+2.9

This method provides an overall measurement of productivity, which management can refer to in evaluating progress. However, the availability of standard man-hours (earned hours) can provide more detailed information for control through the productivity trend control report which is discussed next.

Table 3-4   Productivity Trend Control

	Direct (Productive) Labor				Direct Charged to Indirect (hours)	Total Actual Direct Labor (hours)	Earned to Total Actual Direct (%)
	Earned Hours		Actual Hours	Efficiency (%)			
	Scheduled	Produced					
Period 1							
Total		2608	3348	77.9	5073	8421	31
A		173	200	86.7	175	375	46
B		674	900	74.9	2370	3270	26
C		1349	1664	81.0	1815	3479	40
D		412	584	70.5	713	1297	32
Period 2							
Total		2601	3364	77.3	4649	8013	34
A		164	186	88.2	186	372	44
B		682	928	73.4	2160	3088	22
C		1428	1766	80.8	1560	3326	43
D		327	484	67.6	743	1227	26
Period 3							
Total		3020	3700	81.6	5011	8711	35
A		193	213	90.9	180	393	49
B		1013	1205	84.0	2330	3535	29
C		1222	1493	81.8	1690	3183	38
D		592	789	75.1	811	1600	37
Period 4							
Total		3529	3886	90.8	4407	8293	42
A		200	193	103.7	158	351	57
B		1070	1060	101.0	2129	3189	34
C		1739	1880	92.5	1465	3345	55
D		520	753	69.2	655	1408	37
	(1)	(2)	(3)	(4)	(5)	(6)	

Productivity Trend Control Report

The productivity trend control concept (Table 3-4) demonstrates how productivity can be monitored on a more frequent (weekly, monthly, or quarterly) basis to provide data that is more actionable than the broad overall measurements illustrated in the foregoing examples. The elements of control in this method are:

1. Measurement of hours earned through use of the earned-hour allowance applied to production in each department or cost center.

2. Identification of the amount of direct labor diverted to indirect work.

3. Measurement of efficiency while on standard work.

EXPLANATION OF THE PRODUCTIVITY TREND CONTROL REPORT

The figures included in this report represent actual results in a company using such a report.

Scheduled Earned Hours

The purpose of this column (which is not filled in), is to indicate the desired level of production. A comparison of the scheduled earned hours with the earned hours produced provides information as to the attainment of the production required.

Earned Hours Produced (Column 1)

Production in each of the cost centers has been extended by the standard or earned hours. The earned hours are based on time studies made by industrial engineers.

Actual Hours (Column 2)

This column shows the actual hours of direct labor required to achieve production. A direct comparison can be made of the earned hours with the actual hours.

Percent Efficiency (Column 3)

The earned hours in column 1 are divided by the actual hours in column 2.

Direct Charged to Indirect (Column 4)

This column shows the number of direct labor hours charged to an indirect labor category. Some of the classifications making up this category are: lack of materials, machine breakdown, tools in bad condition, cleaning up, and no standard available.

Total Actual Direct Labor (Column 5)

This column shows the total hours of employees hired to perform direct labor tasks. This is a total of columns 2 and 4.

The philosophy of the company using this report was originally based on a two-pronged approach:

1. Monitoring percent efficiency (column 3).
2. Controlling the amount charged to the indirect category (column 4).

The company found, however, that a dual approach to control tended to dilute the effectiveness of the report. Column 3 in period 4, for example, shows some high percentages of efficiency. Because of this, there was a tendency to downplay the importance of the charges made to the indirect category in column 4.

For this reason management turned to the single indicator of overall efficiency shown in column 6. This was obtained by dividing the earned hours in column 1 by the total actual direct labor hours in column 5.

Note that when this is done, the 103.7% shown for cost center A becomes 57% on an overall basis. The 101.1% for cost center B becomes 34%. The reason for the lower percentages, of course, is that the base for calculating them is broader since it includes all direct labor hours rather than only that portion utilized on standard work.

This does not mean that columns 3 and 4 should no longer be used for control purposes. On the contrary, the information contained in these columns is very helpful in pinpointing the reason for low productivity of labor once the overall indicator identifies the areas requiring immediate attention.

Measurement of productivity is not limited to direct labor alone; total conversion costs should be monitored in a similar manner.

Measurement of Conversion Cost

One approach in monitoring conversion costs is to use the earned hours in each period as a base for determining the conversion cost per earned hour, as is demonstrated in Exhibit 3-1.

Over the four periods, all of which represent an actual company situation, it is noted that there is an inverse relationship between volume, as represented by earned hours, and conversion cost per earned hour.

Note that the total conversion cost per earned hour drops from $7.710 in the first period to $5.609 in the fourth period, while the volume of activity increases from 2608 earned hours in the first period to 3529 in the fourth period.

The most common "impulse" explanation is that this is caused by the fixed portion of conversion costs which become smaller per earned hours as volume increases. This is not true in this case, because the fixed overhead segment of cost in this operation is usually small—too small to have so great an impact.

What causes this behavior, then? To determine the answer to this, note that conversion costs are relatively fixed at $20,000 per period, while earned hours range from 2601 to 3529. (The variation in total dollars of conversion cost is due to changes in product mix.)

Since fixed costs, such as depreciation, rent-equivalent costs, and supervisory labor are not a large segment, direct labor represents the predominant portion of conversion cost. This is characteristic of many labor-intensive operations. Also characteristic of some companies is the tendency to maintain a residual or rounded-out labor force which remains fairly fixed within a certain range of operations. Therefore, as volume increases within a given range of activity, productivity of direct labor also increases.

Not only is direct labor subject to productivity changes as a result of changes in volume, material cost behaves in a similar manner. If

Exhibit 3-1   Conversion Cost Per Earned Hour

	Earned Hours[a]	Total Conversion Cost ($)[b]	Conversion Cost per Earned Hour ($)[c]
Period 1			
Total	2,608	20,106	7.710
A	173	969	5.590
B	674	7,580	11.247
C	1,349	8,405	6.231
D	412	3,152	7.633
Period 2			
Total	2,601	19,297	7.419
A	164	959	5.861
B	682	7,256	10.631
C	1,428	8,150	5.707
D	327	2,932	8.957
Period 3			
Total	3,020	20,991	6.951
A	193	984	5.091
B	1,013	8,342	8.238
C	1,222	7,686	6.289
D	592	3,979	6.713
Period 4			
Total	3,529	19,797	5.609
A	200	898	4.487
B	1,070	7,373	6.889
C	1,739	8,137	4.680
D	520	3,389	6.467

[a] The earned hours are the same as those shown on the productivity trend control report.

[b] Total conversion cost represents all manufacturing costs except material.

[c] Conversion cost per earned hour is calculated by dividing the earned hours into the total conversion cost.

the mix of production remains relatively constant but volume increases, there is a basic amount of material scrap that does not rise in proportion to the increase in volume. In addition, there is a tendency for quality levels to improve when volume is high and runs are not interrupted.

SUMMING UP

Most of the literature on the effect of volume on cost behavior assumes that reduced unit costs are the result of spreading fixed overhead expenses over a broader base.

Rarely, if ever, is it suggested that direct labor and material are affected by the volume of activity. Profit projections therefore can be erroneous if the effect of volume on these two important cost elements is not considered.

The realistic business executive interested in improving his company's profitability must be able to distinguish between productivity resulting from improved methods of manufacture and productivity resulting from increased volume. To blindly use a productivity indicator without recognizing the underlying influences behind it will not assure profitable operations.

CHAPTER 4

DIAGNOSING COMPANY WEAKNESSES AND TAKING CORRECTIVE ACTION

Many medium-sized companies, too large for direct face-to-face communication, too small for elaborate information systems, can benefit enormously from well planned, well guided management meetings. Such meetings can do much to ferret out serious trouble spots for corrective action.

There is no such thing as a degree in being a general manager, executive vice-president, or president. No college course and no series of case studies or seminars adequately provides the top executive with the type of practical information he needs to run his activity. In his position as a key executive, however, he does have at his disposal the best experts in the company in each field—whether it be sales, manufacturing, engineering, or finance. If these functional managers do not prove to be the experts he has assumed them to be, he will soon find out because he must rely upon them for the information he uses in making his decisions.

Although financial indicators can be a very helpful guide to a management interested in improving its competitive position, the analysis of such indicators in abstraction without the participation of the key members of management has only limited benefits.

Team participation is mandatory if good results are to be achieved; it is necessary that key executives be fully aware of the strengths and weaknesses of their company in relation to the industry of which they are a part.

This chapter is devoted to demonstrating how a group of managers can review the operating statement, make comparisons with the industry average, and attempt to determine the reasons their company falls short of meeting the industry average.

Exhibit 4-1 shows the industry averages for a five-year period. The last column shows the equivalent figures for the ABC Company for the most recent year. The general manager of the company has called together the following executives whose titles and first names are:

General manager	Don
Manufacturing manager	Joe
Controller	Jack
Personnel manager	Bob
Sales manager	Harry

GENERAL

MANAGER: "Gentlemen, I have called you together so we can look at ourselves introspectively by comparing the results shown on our financial statement with the results for our industry as shown in Exhibit 4-1 which has been previously distributed to you.

"Through periodic meetings such as this, I hope to promulgate free and open discussion among ourselves as to:

- Where our weak points are in relation to our competitors.
- What we can do to overcome these weaknesses.

"Let's begin by looking at the pretax profit. You will notice that this figure is 8.2% of sales as compared with 12.2% for the industry. Prior to the time we began receiving the industry statistical reports, we thought this was reasonably good—we had some feeling of satisfaction with our performance as managers. The comparison in Exhibit 4-1 referred to earlier points up the fact that we are not quite as good as we have led ourselves to believe. With this as background, let us look at the other items, a line at a time, in an effort to pinpoint some of our problems and possibly reach some meaningful conclusions.

Exhibit 4-1 Financial Ratio Study—ABC Company Compared to the Industry

	Industry Statistics (%)					ABC Company, This Year	
	Four Years Ago	Three Years Ago	Two Years Ago	Last Year	This Year		
Gross sales	103.7	103.8	103.9	103.8	104.0	104.8	
Less returns and allowances	3.7	3.8	3.9	3.8	4.0	4.8	←— "Clean up the 'dirty' orders"
Net sales	100.0	100.0	100.0	100.0	100.0	100.0	
Cost of goods sold							
Material	31.3	35.6	33.9	35.9	36.9	33.9	
Factory labor	13.8	12.1	12.6	9.1	9.0	14.0	←— "Automate!"
Factory overhead	17.7	16.4	17.2	16.2	14.6	16.0	←— "Establish budgets"
Total	62.8	64.1	63.7	61.2	60.5	63.9	
Gross profit	37.2	35.9	36.3	38.8	39.5	36.1	
Selling expenses							
Sales salaries and commissions	7.3	7.9	7.7	7.3	7.8	8.2	←— "Standardize sales compensation methods"
Travel expenses	1.5	1.2	1.2	1.4	1.2	1.3	
Executive and office salaries	4.2	3.9	3.8	3.5	4.5	3.9	
Advertising	1.6	1.3	1.5	1.2	1.5	1.0	
Special promotions	2.1	2.1	2.8	2.6	2.7	3.1	
Total	16.7	16.4	17.0	16.0	17.7	17.5	

Exhibit 4-1 (Continued)

	Industry Statistics (%)					ABC Company This Year	
	Four Years Ago	Three Years Ago	Two Years Ago	Last Year	This Year		
Product development	0.6	0.6	0.5	0.5	0.3	0.0	← "Develop new products"
Administrative expenses							
Executive salaries	2.1	2.4	2.6	2.2	2.2	2.2	
Office salaries	2.4	2.2	1.8	2.4	2.8	2.7	
Nonlabor expenses	5.2	4.9	4.7	5.2	4.4	5.6	← "Oversophistication of computer operations"
Total	9.7	9.5	9.1	9.8	9.4	10.5	
Other income	(1.2)	(0.9)	(0.7)	(0.5)	(0.9)	(0.3)	
Other expenses	1.0	0.8	0.5	0.7	0.8	0.2	
Pretax profit	10.4	9.5	9.9	12.3	12.2	8.2	← "This is where the buck stops"
Finished goods, days	19	16	18	17	16	18	← "Stop overruns—stick to the schedule"
Accounts receivable, days	38	41	39	44	48	52	← "Issue credits promptly"

"Let's look at returns and allowances. This seems to be the customary means of stating the amount of reduction of sales through rebates, defective products, and other reasons that we give credit to customers.

"Joe, as a manufacturing man, I ask you this question: We at the ABC Company show that 4.8% of our sales are returns and allowances—compared with the industry average of 4.0%. The 0.8% may not sound like much, but it is 80¢ out of every \$100 multiplied by the dollars of gross sales. This does become a significant number of dollars over the period of a year."

CONTROLLER: "Let me come to the defense of Joe. This is not quite as bad as it appears. If we inadvertently make a double billing or if we send out two shipments in error, we correct this in the returns and allowances account. Gross sales are thereby automatically reduced through this process. We have recently changed this practice. In the future gross sales will be reduced directly rather than indirectly, and the items shown in returns and allowances will reflect only true allowances and returns."

GENERAL
MANAGER: "I'm certainly glad you have changed the practice. I'd hate to think that a financial statement is being used as an accounting worksheet. If any other kinds of adjustments are being made in the same way, let's clean them up too."

MANUFACTURING
MANAGER: "Some of the returns and allowances can be blamed on 'dirty orders'."

SALES MANAGER: "What do you mean by dirty orders?"

MANUFACTURING
MANAGER: "When an order comes in from the sales department marked 'same as last time,' we pull the order and it frequently turns out that it was not the same as last time, but two times ago. I suggest we prepare some instructions and do a better job of co-

ordinating betweeen sales and manufacturing so we know exactly what to make. This will also help our inventory turnover."

SALES MANAGER: "As far as asking you to make the order the same as last time, I am sure that is the best thing we can do because that is what the customer tells us. However, if we have problems in writing orders, I think we can specify what goes on them. It's only a matter of altering our approach."

MANUFACTURING MANAGER: "Suppose I do this, Harry. I'll have a list made up of all orders that are giving us problems. I'll have this ready for our next meeting so we can all work this out together."

GENERAL MANAGER: "We can do better than that. Would you make a photocopy as the order goes through production control? Bring these copies of all dirty orders to the next meeting so we can deal with specifics. Harry can't just write a memo to his salesmen asking them to write better orders—that's just too general an approach and it will accomplish little."

"So much for dirty orders. Let's move on to cost of goods sold. This is segregated into material, factory labor, and factory overhead. We don't usually have too many bouquets to pass out, but I think you are due one for material. Our material cost is lower than the average for the industry—33.9% of sales as compared with 36.9% for the industry."

CONTROLLER: "There is another factor to be considered before we hand out any bouquets. Our material costs are lower because our TV product line is concentrated more heavily on black and white table models and portables which have a relatively low material content in relation to sales value. Our competitors have more of the stylized, expensive wood cabinets in their lines which have a greater percentage of combination stereo-TV color sets. These have a larger material content and are, incidentally, more profitable. If Harry's salesmen would sell more of these we could increase that profit figure."

PERSONNEL
MANAGER: "I'm a little confused. Even if the table models and portables are less profitable, the material in them is less costly; so doesn't that compensate for the lower price? We sell a lot of them and we put out a good set."

CONTROLLER: "The markup on table models and portables is very low. Even though the material in a color TV-stereo combination is represented by more dollars, the selling price is even greater; so if we could sell more of them, we would come out with a better profit."

SALES MANAGER: "I'd like to sell more of the higher priced line but **every** time I send an order to the factory they goof it up. I got a complaint from a customer only last week that when he switched on the TV the stereo unit began to play. Apparently, our factory is geared up to make the simpler sets; and they do a good job on these—don't get me wrong. I just don't think the more exotic lines are our cup of tea."

MANUFACTURING
MANAGER: "Now just a minute, Harry. Your salesmen send in a small order for combinations about once a month. We can't afford to keep together a group of people familiar with the intracacies of the more exotic items in our line—we have to use people from the lines we run day in and day out. If your department would go out and get some decent-sized orders, I'd set up a special line and train people who would put out a quality product that you'd have no problem selling."

SALES MANAGER: "This is the old story of which came first. We can't sell the product if you can't produce it, and you can't produce it unless we can sell it."

GENERAL
MANAGER: "Maybe we should do some soul searching in this area and develop a marketing program. Harry,

why don't you give Joe an idea of the potential so he can develop some firm plans."

MANUFACTURING
MANAGER:

"Do you have any idea of what this potential really is? It's all well and good to say that we'll try to tap the potential, but I've been stung before. A few years ago, I set up a special line in anticipation of a heavy tape recorder business, but it never materialized and I was left holding the bag."

GENERAL
MANAGER:

"I remember the tape recorder problem—I was a party to it when I was sales manager. If you recall, that was about the time the cartridge-type recorders became very popular. As a result, the conventional product we made took it on the chin. The same thing happened when tape recorders took the place of wire recorders. We profited by that change; in fact that's how we got into the business.

"This is one of the things I hoped would come out of such meetings as this one. It's obvious that we need to do a better job of forward planning and try not to repeat errors of the past. I see Joe's problem—he just can't have specially trained people available to run every small order that comes in the house. We need a plan; we need product selectivity so we can push more of the high profit items rather than just the highly competitive items. The three of us will have to get together in some extended sessions. We'll get some commitment on the part of the sales department in terms of units by product line as well as by dollars and gross margin.

"Then, armed with that type of information, we can get the opinion of the manufacturing department as to needs in terms of people, technology, equipment, and investment in inventory. We can't continue drifting in and out of product lines in a haphazard fashion.

"The next item I want to talk about, gentlemen, is factory labor. I'd like to hear about this from you as personnel manager, Bob. As you can see, factory labor costs are running 14% of sales compared with 9% for the industry. This is five points higher than our competitors. What is the story?"

PERSONNEL
MANAGER:

"I'm going to sound a little like a broken record. As you know, we're in an awfully tight labor market—the likes of which we haven't seen since World War II. Another factor is turnover. It isn't only a matter of losing experienced people and hiring green replacements—we almost always have to hire these new people at higher rates than were paid to the ones we lost."

GENERAL
MANAGER:

"But we're in a distress area with a very high percentage of unemployed."

PERSONNEL
MANAGER:

"True, but the labor pool isn't made up of the type of employees we need. It's the male population that is largely in the ranks of unemployed. But as you know, we need women in our assembly operations for their manual dexterity—and we need inspectors who have a fairly good comprehension of the written word. These types are not available in the quantities we need.

"I do have one suggestion regarding turnover. We have to get closer to our employees so we can become aware of dissatisfactions before they look for other jobs. By the time we find out an employee is looking, it's too late."

MANUFACTURING
MANAGER:

"Who could disagree that we should get closer to our employees. But we could spend all our time wet-nursing 400 employees. There's always going to be some petty bickering that we can never resolve because of personality differences. Arbitrating these differences would take up too much time and accomplish little.

"The way you can make real inroads in the cost

of factory labor—and I've been saying this for three years—is to automate the assembly operations. That's where a good deal of the cost is."

CONTROLLER: "That will require a good deal of investment though."

MANUFACTURING
MANAGER: "Of course it will. But no one seemed to be too concerned about investment when we built that new office building just to house your new computer—air conditioning and all—while my people sweat. There's a way to eliminate a good deal of employee dissatisfaction, Bob. Air condition the factory like our competitors are doing."

CONTROLLER: "But we were able to come up with some savings."

MANUFACTURING
MANAGER: "You'll have to convince me of that. All I see is a lot more reports that I don't have time to read because of all the unnecessary detail they show. I want the big picture, but your computer gives me all the nit-picking detail that I can do without."

GENERAL
MANAGER: "Joe and Jack, let's make the discussion of reports the subject of a separate meeting. Joe, suppose you get together copies of the reports you're talking about and we'll go into them in greater depth.

"Regarding your recommendation for automation, I recall that you did talk about this before, and I have no doubt that you are right. However, as you know, the corporate office requires us to submit a request for appropriation with a calculation or payback—using the discounted cash flow method. I know how you despise paperwork, but we'll have to do it."

MANUFACTURING
MANAGER: "OK, I'll write something up and turn it over to Jack. I know that if I put in an automated line for $100,000 I can make payroll savings in excess of $40,000 per year. After deducting depreciation and maintenance, there will be a net saving of $30,000 per year, or a payback of $3\frac{1}{3}$ years. If this isn't con-

vincing enough and they want to use the discounted cash flow method, I don't understand it—let Jack's computer do it."

GENERAL
MANAGER: "I'm sure Jack will be glad to help you once you give him the basic information. Let's move on to factory overhead. You may be able to throw some light on this one, Jack. Why is our overhead 16% of sales when the industry figures is only 14.6%?"

CONTROLLER: "I believe the major part of this difference is due to the way we handle depreciation. As you know, our equipment is quite new and we use accelerated depreciation in our costing. As far as I can tell, most of our larger competitors have equipment purchased 12 to 15 years ago when prices were lower.

GENERAL
MANAGER: "You're probably right. There should be offsetting effects though—our productivity should be higher with newer equipment."

CONTROLLER: By the way, Joe, when we justified purchase of the new equipment, one of the potential savings was a reduction in the number of maintenance men. We still have as many as we ever did. This is another reason the overhead is up."

MANUFACTURING
MANAGER: "Well, it just seems that everything has been going wrong. We had to use our maintenance crew to make a lot of building repairs."

GENERAL
MANAGER: "I do recall that you were to reduce your crew by five men if we purchased the new equipment. By the way, Jack, your departmental reports don't show budget figures by which we can compare the actual costs to see if they're in line. If you did include a budget based on the annual plan, we could spot these things before too much time gets by us. This is a subject we might discuss after the meeting.

"Let's move into Harry's area now. You'll note

that salesmen's salaries and commissions for the industry—for the entire five years—fall within a single percentage point. There is not a figure below 7% nor one above 8%—which is surprising. In our case this cost is running at 8.2%. Are we paying the men too much? What's the story?"

SALES MANAGER: "Well, Don, as you know, I inherited the sales organization. Some of our men are on compensation plans that include straight commission, salary and commission, salary and bonus, and salary only. One of my goals is to have the entire compensation plan uniform by next year.

"Along with this, you will notice that our executive office salaries are lower than industry. With the standardization of method of payment, I would like to restructure the sales organization to put more management into the field. The combined figure will probably not change but we will look better under salesmen's salaries and commissions and will be a bit higher under sales executives' and office salaries."

GENERAL
MANAGER: "Sounds good to me. This should make the whole organization more effective."

"Let's focus on advertising next. We have spent about 1% of our sales dollar on this item—which is about 30% less than the rest of the industry. Would an increase in this figure result in added volume?"

SALES MANAGER: "I don't believe so. We haven't done too much in institutional advertising because we have no new product to advertise."

GENERAL
MANAGER: "Other companies are glorifying their products through national magazines."

SALES MANAGER: "That's because they have something new. You will see that we're spending a lot of money under special promotions. This is principally sales contests to motivate the salesmen. We do this because our product is at the cheaper end of the line and our men get bored with this sort of thing in a market where others are selling a broader line and glamorizing a variety of models.

"What I would like to do is take the money I am spending on sales contests and put it into product development where we are spending virtually no money. This will be a greater motivation for our sales force. Of course this program will have to be long range. We have to plan on new products, techniques, and new designs for existing products."

GENERAL MANAGER: "This excites me because it fits into the pattern. We have been talking about the fact that we are drifting into new products on a casual basis and not doing a good job because of lack of proper planning and coordination. What you are saying is that we need some specific product development. We can't tell what the outcome will be, but I can see the benefits of closer liaison among sales, product development, and manufacturing."

SALES MANAGER: "We cannot do this for this year and next year and then drop it—the program must go on according to a definite long-range program."

GENERAL MANAGER: "We have already covered product development, so let's skip down to administrative expenses. Jack, I see that we are in good shape on executive salaries and office salaries but we're high on nonlabor expenses. We show 5.6% of sales—which is higher than our competitors in any of the five years. What are we doing here that puts us out of line?"

CONTROLLER: "I guess this is mostly our computer rental. As you know, we're now putting out reports on sales by customer, by territory, and by product, and we're also analyzing commissions by salesmen which we

used to do manually. We're also giving the foremen a daily efficiency report by individual operator so they can nail down inefficiency by operator
and by operation."

MANUFACTURING
MANAGER:

"We can do without these daily efficiency reports.
Each of my foremen gets a stack of paper one inch
high showing this mass of detail. We receive the
report two days late but even if we received it the
next morning it would take each foreman an hour
to review it. Even then, it's too late to take action
on something an operator has long since for-
gotten.

"I can tell how efficient my people are by the
number of TV sets that come off the end of the
line each hour. I can also control poor workmanship by the number of reworks we get at the end of
the line. As soon as we find that a girl is doing a
poor solder job, we know the position on the line
and we take care of the matter immediately—without a stack of paper to tell us. As far as I'm concerned, you can cut out these reports and save the
money."

GENERAL
MANAGER:

"Jack, I know that you and I went into this computer program with high hopes of improving efficiency and saving money. I'm wondering if we
might not have been sold a bill of goods by computer salesmen who would have us spend a dollar
to get ten cents worth of information. Let's take a
good look at this.

"The next item is finished goods. I notice that
we have an 18 days' supply compared with 16 days
for the industry. As you know, this is money. Inventory represents assets that are not turned over.
What is the story on getting this under better control, Harry?"

SALES MANAGER:

"My records show that the factory is overrunning
production schedules. If they stick to the schedule

I request, we would be slightly under the industry."

GENERAL
MANAGER: "Is that true, Joe?"

MANUFACTURING
MANAGER: "Well, you know that when a line is running well
—with very few defects—it's much cheaper to keep
running because when we stop and start up again
later costs go up considerably."

SALES MANAGER: "What good is low cost inventory when you have
to write off a couple hundred thousand dollars at
the end of the model year?"

GENERAL
MANAGER: "Joe, this only reinforces my point. I think that
it's imperative that you, Harry, and I get together
as soon as possible to do some down-to-earth planning. Let's set a definite date before the day is
out.

"The last item I want to cover is accounts receivable. As you can see, we have 52 days of outstanding receivables. Again, we're higher than industry averages. What can we do about it?"

CONTROLLER: "One of the reasons the receivables are so high is
that it takes so long to process credits. I have one
case where a customer won't pay a $5000 bill be-
cause he says he is entitled to a credit for $45 which
hasn't been received.

"I suggest that the salesmen be allowed to ap-
prove credits for $50 or less. A credit still has to be
processed and we have to find out why it is being
requested, but this procedure would help our collection."

SALES MANAGER: "If after the credit has been allowed and a study reveals that it really is the customer's fault, who is
going to bear the cost of that credit? Will it be
charged back to the sales department?"

CONTROLLER: "I don't think that is going to happen very often.
The $50 that we might lose occasionally would be
offset by savings in telephone calls, letter writing,
and ill will."

GENERAL
MANAGER: "I am a little concerned. I think we would have
                              to institute a monitoring system to be sure that
                              salesmen not abuse this system."

SALES MANAGER: "I'll work this out with Jack, and we'll talk it over
                              with you before I issue instructions to my sales
                              people."

GENERAL
MANAGER: "I hope this meeting has been as helpful to you
                              as it has been to me. Just by way of summation,
                              our discussions have highlighted the following
                              areas which require our attention:

                              "We covered the subject of dirty orders which
                              have been a source of confusion to our manufac-
                              turing people and have undoubtedly rankled some
                              of our customers. This meeting permitted us to air
                              the problem which we will explore further with a
                              view toward taking corrective steps.

                              "We also talked about the problems of small
                              orders and about increasing our volume in more
                              profitable lines. Our approach will include a co-
                              ordinated effort among sales, product develop-
                              ment, and manufacturing to come up with a pro-
                              gram for better selectivity in our product line.

                              "The sales compensation plan will be standard-
                              ized and organization shifts made in order to
                              make our field sales effort more effective.

                              "Automation, as a means for reducing factory
                              costs and coping with the labor shortage problems,
                              will be implemented in the foreseeable future.

                              "It's obvious, also, that we have other incon-
                              gruities in our procedures which require further
                              investigation. I refer to the possibility of overly de-
                              tailed reports, the question as to whether or not we
                              have overexpanded our computer facilities, and
                              the problem of issuing credits to customers on a
                              timely basis.

                              "I'm certain that future meetings of this type
                              will put all these problems in proper focus and

facilitate effective solutions. Thank you, gentlemen. I'll notify you of the date of our next meeting."

The foregoing describes a composite of actual happenings at meetings held by several companies. While use of meetings for problem solving is sometimes criticized because they can become a forum for the more vocal members of the group, a well-controlled discussion with specific objectives can be highly productive. The following guidelines will assure greater success.

- Establish a definite agenda of the topics to be covered. In this case the agenda consisted of explanations and solutions to specific out-of-line situations.
- Be alert to the opinions of those in other areas of responsibility who are in a position to flush out deficiencies that might not otherwise be revealed by those directly responsible for the activity.
- Make a definite decision to take certain action. If action cannot be taken, give specific reasons why it cannot. Should further investigation be required, make this known and set definite dates for accomplishment.

The ability to direct a group of executives in the pursuit of reasons for and solutions to problems is one of the marks of business leadership. Diagnosing a business through a team approach certainly calls for the exercise of such leadership. And, as the example in this chapter demonstrates, one way such leadership can be achieved naturally and painlessly lies in framing the questions one wants the answers to first, and then obtaining the benefit of all the best-informed opinions in a frank and open group discussion.

CHAPTER 5

A BACKWARD LOOK AT FORWARD PLANNING

When sound business policies are subordinated to rapid growth, profits suffer and liquidation of past gains is the inevitable result. This chapter describes a pattern that has been typical for many companies, and it recommends a set of guidelines for orderly growth in the form of "ten commandments for expansion."

The desire of management for bigness can be the by-product of a desire for a place in the sun. The bigger the company, the more important the executives of that company become in the business community. Bigness, in this case, is a matter of pride coupled with aggressiveness and ambition.

The needs for bigness can also be ordained by the forces of competition continually squeezing out the marginal producer who does not have the resources to keep up with the growth of technology. This competitive situation forces companies to do more forward planning than they might otherwise do.

It is fortunate that the importance of forward planning is attracting so much management attention. However, because of the emphasis on looking into the future, there is a tendency to discount the importance of past history. This is unfortunate because history frequently contains a wealth of information on past errors in judgment which can be minimized in future planning.

THE CASE OF THE DURARD COMPANY

Take the case of the Durard Plastics Company whose products consist of plastics molding, metal stamping, and related hand assembly operations, The product line includes such items as push buttons for radios, plastic knobs for appliances, plastic bottles with caps, electric shaver parts, small radio cabinets, and a variety of metal parts used in the appliance industry.

The management of this company wanted to increase its share of the market. It planned to achieve this goal through the purchase of established companies as well as expansion from within. As each acquisition was digested, the plan was to move the operations to the town of Durard, for which the parent company was named.

The management of the company was disappointed in progress— and changed general managers three times during a six-year period. The chronology of events leading to management dissatisfaction was as follows:

- *Purchase of Acme Plastics and expansion from within.* Acme Plastics became a part of Durard in August of the first year—as indicated in the pictorial diary represented by Exhibit 5-1. This acquisition resulted in a substantial increase in sales volume, as well as profits. Since plans called for all Acme activities to be moved to Durard, a building expansion program was undertaken. This was completed in the spring of the second year, and the move was made. Concurrently with the completion of this move, 12 injection molding presses were purchased and set up in the expanded plant. The combination of the Acme move and the establishment of an injection molding department proved to be "too big a bite." Since only key supervisory personnel of the Acme Company were transferred, critically needed skills such as setup men and die and mold repairmen were in short supply. Utilization of equipment, which had normally been running at 95%, now dropped to an average of 45 to 50%. The new injection molding presses ran less than 25% of the time for several months following installation while "bugs" were being taken care of and operators and setup men trained.

Naturally, these problems reflected themselves in reduced sales volume as well as reduced profits. As a result, the second year ended with a loss.

Sales slipped throughout the second year because of the company's inability to make shipments to customers. Some improvement was

Exhibit 5-1 DURARD COMPANY ACTUAL AND PROJECTED SALES FOR TEN YEAR PERIOD

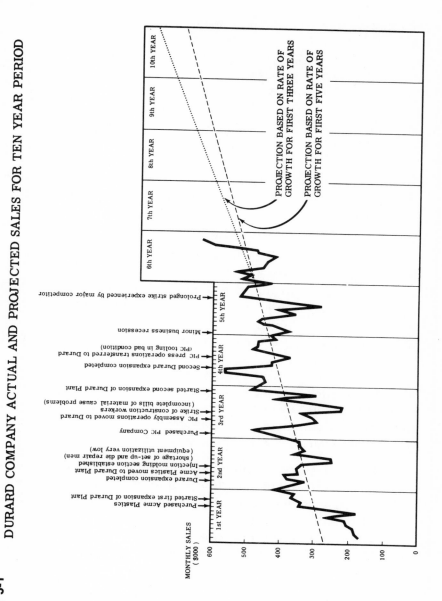

experienced during the third year. Utilization of the equipment transferred from Acme increased to 75%—somewhat short of the desired 90 to 95%. The newly purchased injection molding equipment still lagged at 65% rather than at the desired level. The company anticipated it would take from six to nine months more before utilization of the equipment could attain optimum levels. The profit outlook still was not good, but improvement seemed in sight. Because the Durard Company was in sound financial condition, it was able to weather the storm. Under similar conditions other companies would have failed.

- *Purchase of the PIC Company.* The general manager, who had been with Durard two years, had been released and replaced by a new man. The new man was advised of the company's interest in growth and of the recent problems that had been encountered.

Shortly after taking over, the new general manager learned that the PIC Company, which was in financial straits and losing money, could be purchased at a bargain price. This purchase would permit Durard to immediately get into another related product line and pick up PIC's customers. With the Acme move out of the way, the decision was made to purchase PIC and to transfer the operations to Durard as soon as possible.

Within two months, the unprofitable hand assembly items were moved. It was felt that the high labor rates paid at PIC's present location made profits out of the question. The substantially lower rates in the Durard area should help considerably. Although the rates were lower, management miscalculated on two other counts:

1. Purchasing and production scheduling personnel were unfamiliar with the new product line. Bills of material were incomplete because PIC personnel had kept this information "in their heads" rather than on documented records.

2. The Durard plant could not accommodate the PIC press operations. The trouble was not lack of space but the wrong type of floor construction—PIC's heavy presses required heavily reinforced floors.

PIC press operators and tool shopmen were leaving as soon as they could find other employment—knowing that their tenure was limited.

Downtime on presses, because of shortage of skilled personnel, increased astronomically. Plans for the second Durard expansion were hurriedly made, but actual work could not start because of an unexpected strike which closed down all construction in the area. Finally, with the settlement of the strike, construction began late in the year. Durard made a small profit that year, but its working capital was becoming strained.

The second expansion was completed late in spring of the fourth year. Production schedules were firmed up and certain PIC items were now running at high volume. But then problems began to mount again. The tools used at PIC were of a poor quality—no longer meeting the tighter requirements of the industry, which had greatly increased the use of automated assembly equipment. As a result, many fabricated parts that did not meet the greater tolerances required had to be scrapped or reworked. It was obvious that a substantial retooling program was required. In the meantime productivity dropped and production schedules had to be "juggled" frequently to satisfy specific customer demands. The tooling program would require from 15 to 18 months before it could be completed. In the meantime production output continued to drop with the resultant slippage in sales and profits. To add to the problems, a business recession developed near the end of the fourth year during what was normally a high volume production period. Although the recession was relatively mild, productivity continued to slip while the company frantically tried to find competent toolmakers to speed up the retooling program. At this point the general manager was relieved of his responsibilities and still another new man brought in.

The new general manager (let us call him Norm Bayard) was somewhat surprised to learn that his predecessors had such short tenures. He realized that if he mechanically picked up the reins, without some deeper investigation, he might fall victim to the same problems that resulted in the release of his predecessors.

In his "get acquainted" interviews with the members of his staff, he decided that he would attempt to determine exactly what the problems were and how they might have been prevented—or at least greatly minimized. He sensed that some of the staff would undoubtedly, in the role of "Monday morning quarterbacks," apply the 20/20 vision of hindsight to impress the new boss. To avoid being misled Norm double-checked all statements that were made. When he was told that bad tools had been at fault, he asked such questions as:

- Were the tools poorly designed or were they merely worn out and in need of maintenance?
- Could better maintenance have prevented the problem?
- Is it possible that only some of the key high volume tools were the source of the problems? In that case would the availability of a duplicate set of tools have allowed for the needed maintenance?

By asking questions such as these, statements could be pinned down to more factual data. Without being obvious, Norm gradually accumulated a "bank" of information which was correlated with past sales. To this he added the data accumulated during his own tenure. Exhibit 5–1 was then prepared. Since growth was being emphasized by the company, two projections were made for the balance of the 10-year period. These were based on:

- Rate of growth for the first three years.
- Rate of growth for the first five years.

The first three years would project the trend if the high rate of sales increase experienced in the first three years could be duplicated. The five-year period, however, was a more conservative estimate because it reflected the problems incident to the PIC move and the effect of a business recession. The favorable effect of a major competitor's strike, which occurred in the sixth year, was not included because this was considered to be a nonrecurring "windfall."

A PERIOD OF CONSOLIDATION

Corrective programs instituted by Norm and his predecessor gradually began to take hold. Although production volume continued to slip, defective production was reduced considerably. It was now only a matter of time before the problems of tooling and setup would be corrected. The Durard Company had profited immensely from the long strike of its competitor because it was able to take business on a more selective basis and set up certain equipment to run continuously, day in and day out. One-shift operations were expanded to two shifts, and the work week was extended to 45 hours. Sales and profits soared—somewhat relieving a serious shortage of working capital.

THE TEN COMMANDMENTS FOR PROFITABLE EXPANSION

Norm felt that the pictorial diary of problems experienced by the Durard Company, which are depicted in Exhibit 5-1, could serve a twofold purpose:

1. It would provide a history of past events and demonstrate their effect on operations.
2. The availability of this type of data would be helpful at management meetings to reinforce the need for solid planning.

It seemed that the previous two general managers moved too quickly to fulfil the company's desire for growth—with the result that the company's working capital became seriously impaired. As a result of this and the other observations made by Norm, the following "ten commandments for expansion" were established:

1. Expand in your own field of expertise. Competition is tough enough without giving your competitors a built-in advantage.
2. Evaluate the market potential before expanding. Check the life cycle of your products to assure that you don't find yourself making a horse-and-buggy product in the automotive age.
3. Check possible monopoly restrictions. There is no point in expanding and then going through divestiture proceedings.
4. Evaluate your financial resources. Determine the potential effect on working capital if things don't go according to plan.
5. Check what your competitors are doing. If they have already embarked on a major expansion program, you may want to take a different course to avoid a large investment in excess facilities of that particular product.

6. Don't expand just for the sake of size. Nothing is to be gained by increasing sales at the sacrifice of profits.

7. Coordinate engineering and production activities. Make certain that bills of material and process specifications are documented rather than being kept in someone's head. This applies to nonmanufacturing activities with equal force.

8. If the design of a product is changed, modify the tooling immediately. Waiting until the order is processed can mean expensive delays and problems in scheduling.

9. Don't expand beyond the limits of available skills. Hold expansion within the limits of the skills that can be made available in the foreseeable future, otherwise efficiency and utilization of equipment will suffer.

10. Transfer the required skills—hourly as well as salaried. If some employees are reluctant to relocate, ask them to stay on for an additional six-month period to train employees at the new location. The extra travel and living expenses will be far cheaper in the long run.

The company recognized that its policies emphasizing growth had been taken too literally by past general managers. To avoid a recurrence, the ten commandments were summarized in the form of a policy letter to all members of management. All subsequent plans for expansion were reviewed by a committee headed by the executive vice-president and made up of representatives of the following divisions: operations, engineering, sales, and finance. This group met once a month to evaluate plans for future expansion and to review progress on current moves. The results of these meetings were summarized and presented to the officers of the company for review.

Establishment of the ten commandments and the monthly reviews had a salutory effect. The rate of growth for the balance of the 10-year period was not as great as the company had hoped for originally. However, the rate did exceed the growth pace of the first five-year period. The growth of profits, however, tripled the rate of the first five years.

The experience of the Durard Company provides an object lesson for other companies intent on rapid growth. The question they should ask is: "Am I interested in rapid expansion of sales volume or am I interested in more profits?" It may be more judicious, for reasons outlined in this chapter, to slow down the rate of sales growth in order to maximize profits.

Assuring Profitable Operations

CHAPTER 6

FOCUSING ON THE BIG PICTURE

A well thought-out profit plan allows management to evaluate the various probabilities and alternatives in advance. Then, when things go "off course," management will already have had its "fire drills" and will be far better equipped to cope with the unforeseen.

Far too often, discussions with executives of troubled businesses reveal vagueness as to management plans for the coming year. The sales department of such a company more than likely expresses the opinion that sales expectations for the coming year will change by x percent, without a clear insight as to the underlying factors in the market. The production executives in turn point out that their production plans depend entirely on sales orders, so they must remain "loose" in their plans. First-line supervisors may have no idea of management's plans or goals—their efforts being adjusted from day to day as they receive new bits of information on the latest management thinking. In short, many companies operate today's mass production facilities on a job shop basis.

A modern-day business, with its heavy capital and human resource requirements cannot afford to "drift"—formulating its plans in a haphazard way as surrounding pressures dictate.

In originally getting into the business, it was necessary to establish definite plans. Underwriters would not provide funding unless they saw a clear-cut plan of action and were assured that the company would develop along orderly lines. So in operating a going business, a plan of action with definite profit goals is imperative.

Although the goals in a profit plan may not always materialize, the procedures required in the development of a plan provide a kind of simulation wherein the various probabilities and alternatives are evaluated in advance. Then, when things go wrong, management will already have had its "fire drills" and will be far better equipped to cope with the unforeseen.

LOOKING AT THE NEW YEAR

The HiFi-Stereo Corporation (a fictitious company) provides an illustration of the importance one company placed on "planning for profits." This company manufactured a line of products that had become increasingly popular with the "music crowd." Its sales had been running at about $8,000,000 per year. While its own pretax profit on sales had been averaging 8%, competitors had been enjoying 10%. The executives of this company felt that their plans should be predicated on realization of profits at least as good as the 10% average for the industry.

In an effort to improve the coming year's results, the market potential and the company's profit goals were carefully evaluated. Examination of the balance sheet showed the stockholder equity to be $3,375,000. Industry statistics indicated that competitors turned their equity $2\frac{1}{2}$ times a year in terms of sales. This meant that HiFi-Stereo, to match industry turnover of investment, must achieve a sales volume of $8,437,500 annually ($3,375,000 $\times$ $2\frac{1}{2}$ turns). If, in addition to matching industry turns of investment, the company also matches the 10% profit on sales, it will realize a 25% return on its investment (10% $\times$ $2\frac{1}{2}$ turns).

The 25% return on investment became the goal for the new year. The company management was careful to spell out that attainment of this goal was predicated on two factors:

1. Obtaining a sales volume of at least $8,437,500.
2. Realizing a pretax profit of 10% on these sales.

In assessing its ability to attain the required sales volume, the sales department analyzed its territories and customers to determine realistically the volume that could be achieved for the coming year.

Although a market analysis in depth gave assurance that a sales level of $8,308,000 was attainable, the company could not achieve the desired $8,437,500 unless it added a new product to its line. The most likely candidate was a low-priced stereo unit (model DI) selling for $60 each. This item had just come onto the market and appeared to have a good potential because of its convenient size. Although there was a good chance that the company could sell approximately $500,000, it was recognized that market tests had not yet been completed (the item was just off the drawing board and a few dozen prototypes were being field tested). Since only $129,700 in sales was needed to attain the "magic volume" of $8,437,500, the company decided to take a calculated risk and assume that field test results would be sufficiently well received to permit this volume of sales of the new product to be made by the end of the coming year.

Going ahead on this assumption, the company next turned its attention to the manufacturing budget. Since selling and administrative expenses had been budgeted at 20% of sales, the factory must provide a 30% gross profit to attain a pretax profit of 10%.

DEVELOPING THE FACTORY BUDGET

The first step in coming up with a budget for control of manufacturing costs is the determination of the level of production. Beginning inventories as well as the desired level of ending inventories are factors that must be taken into account. In projecting the anticipated volume of production, the HiFi-Stereo Corporation did not have to be concerned with beginning inventories because it followed the practice of disposing of previous years' models through discount outlets in noncompetitive selling territories. The production volume for budgeting purposes, then, was the same as the sales forecast. A summary of sales by products is shown in Table 6-1.

These projected sales were given to the manufacturing manager with a request to come up with a budget that would produce a 30% gross profit. He in turn had his scheduling department determine the manufacturing needs by months. In instances in which several products used a common part, arrangements were made to produce these

Table 6-1   Projected Sales

Product	Units	Unit Price ($)	Total Sales ($)
202	20,300	122	2,484,500
610	3,350	150	498,600
707	3,150	275	867,400
810	1,900	596	1,132,900
FO	11,000	150	1,649,100
J2	7,000	197	1,379,700
P6	287	1,030	295,600
DI	2,160	60	129,700
			8,437,500

parts in a single rather than multiple runs. Direct labor and overhead requirements were also evaluated on the basis of monthly requirements to fulfill the sales projection.

PRODUCTION COST REPORT

Upon completion the budget projection was summarized on a production cost report form similar to a form used for the monthly reporting of manufacturing costs against an allowance based on the month's production volume. This form is illustrated in Exhibit 6-1.

The first page of the production cost report provides the big picture of the month and the year-to-date cost. The major elements are summarized for the current month and for the accumulation for the year, including the current month.

In the lower section of the same page is shown the percentage that each of the cost elements is of the estimated sales value of production. The word "estimated" is used because there may be a build-up of component parts over and above the finished units transferred to the finished goods stockroom. These percentages ca n be helpful in ascertaining changes in the "mix" of production. If material as a percentage of sales value is significantly different than the year-to-date percentage, it shows a basic change in the makeup of production going through the plant that month. It may be that conversion costs (labor and overhead) in the products being made are greater and therefore have a larger profit potential than other products in which material cost is a larger factor. (Theoretically, larger profits are made on converting rather than handling material, therefore a month in which products manufactured show a high conversion cost percentage could mean a more profitable product mix.) While study of the production schedule reveals what is being manufactured, the production cost report serves to convert the production schedule into dollar costs by element of cost.

Page 2 of the report summarizes in greater detail the material, direct labor, and indirect labor in the production departments. The material breakdown shows the dollar value of steel used during the month, of purchased fabricated parts, and of purchased components. A constant evaluation of the value of purchased fabricated parts can give a clue as to whether the company should look into expanding its own press section. Direct labor, as well as indirect labor, is broken down by production department. Frequently, a rising trend in the assembly section can furnish a clue that a backlog of fabricated parts and subassemblies is being cleaned up through conversion into finished units. However, if the volume of assembly effort is on the decline, it is possible that there may be a glut of fabricated parts awaiting assembly.

Page 3 shows indirect labor in the service departments, as well as labor-connected expenses. The breakdown by department provides a means for evaluating a possible rising trend by comparing the current month with year-to-date figures (as well as with the budgeted allowance). While labor is broken down by department, labor-connected expenses are shown by expense category.

Page 4 lists the various nonlabor manufacturing expenses by expense category.

The philosophy of the report in providing the big picture to the plant manager emphasizes the natural controllable level of expenses. Material, for example, is controlled by the steel used, by fabricated parts that are purchased, or components that may be bought. Naturally, more refined controls are used at the lower level of management.

The plant manager looks at labor controls by department. But when evaluating labor-connected expenses, he is more interested in

Exhibit 6-1

PRODUCTION COST REPORT

BUDGET PROJECTION FOR YEAR
Month _____ 19 ____

Plant _____

Summary	Month		Year to Date	
	Actual	Allowance	Actual	Allowance
Sales Value of Production				8,437,500
Material		— — —		3,663,040
Direct Labor				724,623
Total Material and Labor				4,387,663
Indirect Labor-Prod'n Depts.	— — —			128,560
Indirect Labor-Service Depts.				398,057
Labor Connected Expenses				284,327
Manufacturing Expenses	—			522,200
Total Overhead				1,333,144
TOTAL COST OF PRODUCTION				5,720,807

OPERATING STATISTICS	% OF TOTAL	% OF TOTAL	% OF TOTAL	% OF TOTAL
Sales Value of Production				100.0
Material				43.4
Direct Labor				8.6
Indirect Labor-Prod'n Depts.				1.5
Indirect Labor-Service Depts.				4.7
Labor Connected Expenses				3.4
Manufacturing Expenses				6.2
TOTAL COST OF PRODUCTION				67.8

COMMENTS:

NO. DAYS WORKED_____

DATE ISSUED_____

70

Plant _____   MATERIAL

Month _____19____

Dept. No.		Month		Year to Date	
		Actual	Allowance	Actual	Allowance
	Steel				381,269
	Purchased fabricated parts				719,669
	Purchased components				2,562,102
	TOTAL MATERIAL COST				3,663,040

DIRECT LABOR

Dept. No.	Department	No. Emp.	Month		Year to Date	
			Actual	Allowance	Actual	Allowance
10	Semi Automatic Press Section					283,151
20	Automatic Press Section					215,646
30	Assembly Section					225,826
	TOTAL DIRECT LABOR COST					724,623

INDIRECT LABOR – PRODUCTION DEPARTMENTS

Dept. No.	Department	No. Emp.	Month		Year to Date	
			Actual	Allowance	Actual	Allowance
10	Semi Automatic Press Section					35,712
20	Automatic Press Section					54,465
30	Assembly Section					38,383
	TOTAL INDIRECT LABOR-PROD'N					128,560

Exhibit 6-1 *(Continued)*

INDIRECT LABOR – SERVICE DEPARTMENTS

Plant _____

BUDGET PROJECTION FOR YEAR
Month _____ 19 ____

Dept. No.	Department	No. Emp.	Month		Year to Date	
			Actual	Allowance	Actual	Allowance
40	General Manager's Staff	4				50,932
42	Personnel	4				32,300
44	Cost Accounting	4				35,070
46	Material Control	7				59,879
48	Engineering	6				45,356
50	Quality Assurance	3				29,585
52	Purchasing	4				29,778
54	Maintenance	10				57,350
60	Receiving and Shipping	12				57,807
	TOTAL					398,057

LABOR CONNECTED EXPENSES

Acct. No	Account Name		Month		Year to Date	
			Actual	Allowance	Actual	Allowance
31	Overtime Premium					37,956
33	Shift Premium					8,986
81	Vacation Expense					24,041
83	Unemployment Insurance					26,352
91	Group Life Insurance					11,000
92	Hospitalization					31,500
93	Pension Expense					38,500
95	Comp. and Liability Ins.					23,000
96	Payroll Taxes					82,992
	TOTAL LABOR CONNECTED					284,327

MANUFACTURING EXPENSE

Plant _____

Acct. No.	Account Name	Month		Year to Date	
		Actual	Allowance	Actual	Allowance
	UTILITIES				
	Water				
	Gas				4,000
	Electricity				4,100
	Telephone				44,300
	Acetylene				9,120
					275
	FACILITIES COSTS				
	Rent				
	Property Taxes				1,000
	Guard Service				8,290
	Cleaning Services				8,200
	Depreciation				11,800
	Insurance				201,000
	Fuel Oil				2,817
					32,500
	SUPPLIES				
	Stationery				
	Postage				5,900
	Expendable Tools				3,100
	Maintenance Material				20,700
	Lubricants and Chemicals				69,000
	Factory Supplies				8,000
	Amortization of dies				4,200
					58,648
	OFFICE EXPENSES				
	Employment Expense-Agencies				
	Subscriptions				4,750
	Dues & Memberships				500
	Computer Service				500
	Rental of Equipment				3,500
	Travel Expense				6,800
					9,200
	TOTAL MANUFACTURING EXPENSE				522,200

73

knowing the category of expense being incurred. By knowing that total unemployment insurance is trending higher, he is alerted to the cost of frequent layoffs and cutbacks. Also, in his dealings with unions, he must have the big picture that tells him the cost of these labor-connected expenses since they loom larger and larger in each new labor contract.

The same principle of identifying labor-connected expenses by expense account primarily and by department secondarily holds for nonlabor manufacturing expenses. The manager should be aware of the total expenditure for expendable tools and maintenance materials, for example. This provides him with overall trend information on major items of cost.

Exhibit 6-1 summarizes the various segments of manufacturing cost as they have been budgeted for the sales volume of $8,437,500. These costs amount to $5,720,807 and reflect a gross profit of 32.2% on sales. This 32.2% must now be analyzed by product line.

GROSS PROFIT BY PRODUCT LINE

The product line analysis illustrated in Exhibit 6-2 is merely a recapitulation of the costs shown in the production cost report. This type of presentation is helpful to nonfinance operating managers in reconciling costs in the budget with the effect of these costs on profitability by product line.

When factory management can see the impact of the costs it generates on the profitability of the products it makes, the figures "come alive" because they take on new meaning.

HOW THE FIGURES ARE BROKEN DOWN BY PRODUCT

Material costs were obtained by extending the quantities of the various products by the required amount of material shown on bills of material prepared by the engineering department. To these requirements allowances were added to provide for a reasonable amount of scrap and spoilage.

The direct labor allowances were based on time studies made by

Exhibit 6-2 Breakdown of Budgeted Production Costs by Product Line

	202	610	707	810	F0	J2	P6	DI	Total
Sales value of production									
Dollars	$2,484,500	498,600	867,400	1,132,900	1,649,100	1,379,700	295,600	129,700	$8,437,500
Units	20,300	3,350	3,150	1,900	11,000	7,000	287	2,160	
Unit price (rounded)	122	150	275	596	150	197	1,030	60	
Material									
Steel	$ 84,751	2,169	21,323	103,806	53,210	96,746	2,818	16,446	$ 381,269
Purchased fabricated parts	135,063	104,925	283,203	80,435	—	27,694	74,344	14,005	719,669
Purchased components	872,126	148,897	152,969	229,440	769,580	328,342	49,938	10,810	2,562,102
Total material	1,091,940	255,991	457,495	413,681	822,790	452,782	127,100	41,261	3,663,040
Direct labor									
Semiautomatic press	$ 31,252	8,767	22,852	136,103	23,106	43,781	1,306	15,984	$ 283,151
Automatic press section	67,591	640	14,541	10,804	41,789	67,607	10,833	1,841	215,646
Assembly	60,929	16,574	33,112	41,799	31,422	28,788	6,759	6,443	225,826
Total direct labor	$ 159,772	25,981	70,505	188,706	96,317	140,176	18,898	24,268	$ 724,623
Total overhead	308,313	46,963	128,386	328,738	182,857	260,440	31,208	46,239	$1,333,144
Total manufacturing cost	$1,560,025	328,935	656,386	931,125	1,101,964	853,398	177,206	111,768	$5,720,807
Gross profit (%)	37.2	34.1	24.3	17.7	33.2	38.1	40.1	13.8	32.2

industrial engineers. Here too, normal allowances for unavoidable delays and other downtime were added so that labor costs would be reasonable and yet realistically attainable.

Overhead was assigned to the product in two ways:

1. Machine-hour rates were applied to hours of machine time for the various presses. The direct labor cost was included as part of this rate.
2. In the assembly section overhead was added to the product through a rate applied to labor-hours required to assemble the product. Labor-hours represented allowed hours rather than the hours actually required for assembly.

After the material, direct labor, and overhead requirements for each of the products was determined, the total manufacturing cost of each product was subtracted from the projected sales to arrive at the gross profit by product. This profit was then divided by the sales to arrive at the gross profit percentage. These percentages are summarized in Table 6-2 in order of profitability.

While the overall profitability of 32.2% of sales is greater than the desired 30%, it is obvious that if sales of products 707, 810, and DI increase and sales of the more profitable items decrease, the actual profit realized could be below the required 30% even if sales of $8,437,500 are attained.

Since the foregoing computations were based on full absorption of

Table 6-2   Gross Profit Percentages in Descending Order

Product	Gross Profit (%)
P6	40.1
J2	38.1
202	37.2
610	34.1
FO	33.2
707	24.3
810	17.7
DI	13.8
Total	32.2

overhead, the HiFi-Stereo Corporation management also used the marginal contribution approach in the determination of the relative profitability of various products. Exhibit 6-3 was prepared with this purpose in mind.

THE MARGINAL CONTRIBUTION APPROACH

Since the concept of marginal contribution is based on the separation of fixed and variable costs, the first step was to determine which of the manufacturing costs should be considered variable with changes in the volume of production and which remain relatively fixed.

Material and direct labor costs were considered to be completely variable with volume. In the overhead segment items listed in Table 6-3 were considered to be variable:

Table 6-3   Variable Overhead Costs

Item	Cost ($)
Labor-connected expenses associated with direct labor	100,000
Expendable tools	20,700
Maintenance materials	69,000
Lubricants and chemicals	8,000
Factory supplies	4,200
Amortization of dies	58,648
Total	260,548

Although some segments of indirect labor in production departments can be considered to be variable, in this case all indirect labor in both the production and service departments was considered to be fixed within a range of $8,000,000 to $10,000,000 in sales volume. Labor-connected expenses applicable to indirect labor and the remaining nonlabor manufacturing expenses were considered to be fixed. A breakdown of the total manufacturing cost of $5,720,807 into its variable and fixed segments is shown in Table 6-4.

The next step was to make a distribution by products. In Exhibit 6-3 the projected sales volume for each product was considered as

Exhibit 6-3 Elements of Budgeted Production Cost As A Percent of Projected Sales

Products	Sales Dollars	Sales Per cent	Material Dollars	Material Per cent	Direct Labor Dollars	Direct Labor Per cent	Variable Overhead Dollars	Variable Overhead Per cent	Total Variable Costs Dollars	Total Variable Costs Per cent	Marginal Contribution (%)	Fixed Overhead Dollars	Fixed Overhead Per cent	Total Manufacturing Cost Dollars	Total Manufacturing Cost Per cent	Gross Profit (%)
P6	295,600	100.0	127,100	43.0	18,898	6.4	6,800	2.3	152,798	51.7	48.3	24,408	8.2	177,206	59.9	40.1
J2	1,379,700	100.0	452,782	32.8	140,176	10.2	50,400	3.7	643,358	46.7	53.3	210,040	15.2	853,398	61.9	38.1
202	2,484,500	100.0	1,091,940	44.0	159,772	6.4	57,600	2.3	1,309,312	52.7	47.3	250,713	10.1	1,560,025	62.8	37.2
610	498,600	100.0	255,991	51.3	25,981	5.2	9,400	1.9	291,372	58.4	41.6	37,563	7.5	328,935	65.9	34.1
FO	1,649,100	100.0	822,790	49.9	96,317	5.8	34,600	2.1	953,707	57.8	42.2	148,257	9.0	1,101,964	66.8	33.2
707	867,400	100.0	457,495	52.7	70,505	8.1	25,600	3.0	553,600	63.8	36.2	102,786	11.9	656,386	75.7	24.3
810	1,132,900	100.0	413,681	36.5	188,706	16.7	67,548	6.1	669,935	59.3	40.7	261,190	23.0	931,125	82.3	17.7
DI	129,700	100.0	41,261	31.8	24,268	18.7	8,600	6.7	74,129	57.2	42.8	37,639	29.0	111,768	86.2	13.8
Total	8,437,500	100.0	3,663,040	43.4	724,623	8.6	260,548	3.1	4,648,211	55.1	44.9	1,072,596	12.7	5,720,807	67.8	32.2

Table 6-4   Breakdown of Total Manufacturing Cost into Fixed and Variable Segments

	Variable ($)	Fixed ($)	Total ($)
Material	3,663,040		3,663,040
Direct labor	724,623		724,623
Indirect labor, Production		128,560	128,560
Indirect labor, Service		398,057	398,057
Labor-connected expenses	100,000	184,327	284,327
Manufacturing expenses	160,548	361,652	522,200
Total manufacturing cost	4,648,211	1,072,596	5,720,807

100%. For analytical purposes variable costs are broken down by material, direct labor, and overhead. This could be helpful in determining whether any of the products is unusually heavy in any of the elements of cost. If, for example, labor looms large, it may be possible to automate in order to reduce labor costs. If material costs are unusually high, it may be possible to redesign the product to simplify the circuitry.

The column listing total variable costs shows the percentage that variable costs are of the total sales for each product. The difference between these percentages and 100% shows the marginal contribution percentage—the percentage of the sales dollar left to cover fixed manufacturing costs, selling, general and administrative expenses, and profits.

For purposes of showing the whole picture so that the marginal contribution percentage can be reconciled to the gross profit percentage, fixed manufacturing costs have been included. The last column in the exhibit lists the gross profit percentages. For convenience of comparison, both the marginal contribution and gross profit percentages are listed in Table 6-5.

Although major differences in profitability of products are obvious, the two figures are not expressed in the same common denominator— as evidenced by the weighted average which is 44.9% on the one hand and 32.2% on the other. To convert the figures to a comparable basis, the marginal contribution percentages for the various products were divided by their average, 44.9%. The gross profit percentages for each of the products were likewise divided by their average, 32.2.

Table 6-5   Comparison of Marginal Contribution and Gross Profit Percentages

Product	Marginal Contribution (%)[a]	Gross Profit (%)
P6	48.3	40.1
J2	53.3	38.1
202	47.3	37.2
610	41.6	34.1
FO	42.2	33.2
707	36.2	24.3
810	40.7	17.7
DI	42.8	13.8
	44.9	32.2

[a] Only manufacturing costs considered.

Thus both columns of figures were expressed in terms of an average equivalent to 100%. The adjusted percentages are shown in Table 6-6.

With the profitability of the eight products expressed in terms of an average represented by 100% in both cases, it was possible to compare marginal contribution percentages directly with gross profit percentages.

Table 6-6   Converting Both Percentages to a Common Denominator

Product	Marginal Contribution (%)[a]	Gross Profit (%)[a]
P6	108	125
J2	119	118
202	105	116
610	93	106
FO	94	103
707	81	75
810	90	55
DI	95	43
	100	100

[a] Only manufacturing costs considered.

In reviewing the gross profit column, management had been concerned with the poor showing of the 810 and DI products because the profitability was about half that of the average—55% for product 810 and 43% for product DI. However, under the marginal contribution percentages, these two products showed a profitability of 90 and 95%, respectively, much closer to the average. In fact, the spread of percentages was much narrower in the marginal contribution column than in the gross profit column. Under the former, the spread ranged from 81 to 119%, while for gross profit the range was 43 to 125%. In the first case the spread was 38 points from the lowest to the highest, while in the second it was 82 points. It was also noted that under the marginal contribution approach three of the eight products showed higher than average profitability, while five showed lower than average. In the gross profit column, the reverse was true— five products were more profitable than average and three less profitable.

These differences between the two methods of measuring profitability were obviously due to the effect of the fixed costs included in the eight products.

While some of these fixed costs were of a "general purpose" nature, such as the personnel department, cost accounting, and the general manager's staff, there were enough other fixed costs that were directly associated with a cost center to warrant further investigation into profitability based on the inclusion of fixed costs specifically applicable to certain products. Since the low profitability of products 810 and DI was evident, the study was concentrated on them.

A review of the product routing sheets with an industrial engineer disclosed that these two products required a number of parts that were fabricated on slower semiautomatic presses. These particular presses were large and even more expensive than some of the fully automatic types. Also, because they were slow large storage areas were required to accumulate the fabricated parts until an optimum-sized batch could be readied to put through the plating department. Because the presses were not automatic they required full time operators —causing labor costs as well as fixed overhead to be high.

If the introduction of product DI is successful and a sales volume of $750,000 to $1,000,000 develops, the company could justify the purchase of additional high speed automatic presses which would reduce labor costs as well as unit fixed costs. In addition, several thousand square feet of factory space would be released for storage of finished goods with a saving in rental for outside facilities. The obsolete presses would have a ready sale in the used machinery market because of a fairly large demand for this type of press. These savings could increase the gross profit to about 32% for both items.

While the main focus was on products 810 and DI, it was noted that product 707, the third product of below-average profitability, also utilized parts made on the slower presses—but not to as great an extent. While labor and overhead savings did not offer as great a potential, material did. A study by the engineers showed that the present model of the 707 used a fair number of vacuum tubes, while competitors were using the newer semiconductors. Although a design change could not be implemented until the next model year, the estimated savings from such a change could reduce material costs from 52.7% of sales to approximately 47%, with a resultant rise in the gross profit percentage from 24.3 to approximately 30%.

In the course of this review of the profit plan, cost reduction recommendations were made for other products in the line. Management recognized that there were additional possibilities for savings. However, they also recognized that a concentration on the three "losers" would provide the greatest savings in the shortest time.

COST REDUCTION RESULTING FROM THE PLAN

The course of action that was adopted consisted of the following:

- Cost reduction efforts were concentrated on products DI, 810, and 707.
- Automated press equipment was ordered without delay because of lead time requirements. If field tests indicated that product DI was successfully field tested and that sufficient sales volume would materialize, the order for the presses would stand. If not, it would be cancelled and alternative solutions sought.
- Redesign of the 707 was also started by replacement of a number of vacuum tubes with semiconductor devices—a change competitors had implemented some time ago. The engineering manager

was instructed also to be alert to the possibility of standardizing sections of the circuitry to facilitate use of an interchangeable printed circuit which could be used on other products.

- Even though there was a possibility that these cost reduction projects could yield some savings within the period being budgeted, no adjustments were made. The manufacturing manager was being held to 32.2% gross profit—barring unforeseen price changes, of course, and unfavorable changes in mix.

A carefully prepared profit plan reconstructs in advance the anticipated happenings of the coming year. It provides the management of a company with a "preview" of things to come as well as an opportunity to make the changes required in order to maximize profitability.

Although the foregoing cost reductions relate to the HiFi-Stereo Corporation, the principle that has been demonstrated is applicable to most companies following this concept of profit planning.

Some managements are reluctant to reveal sales and profit information to factory management. The argument advanced is that the factory should be held accountable only for meeting its budget rather than having profit responsibility. While this can be supported from an academic point of view, it tends to relegate the factory manager to second-class status in the organization. In this era of sharp competition and emphasis on motivation, no stone can be left unturned in the search for innovative ideas which can emanate only from an enthusiastic group of managers who are allowed to participate in the forming of the big picture.

CHAPTER 7

HOW COST MEASUREMENT
TECHNIQUES CAN IMPROVE PROFITS

Plans for the new year are frequently impeded because of delays in forecasting sales. This chapter explains how flexible budget techniques can be employed in minimizing the effect of such delays. It also emphasizes that formalization of a flexible budget can be a highly informative tool to key executives—leading to important cost savings.

Preparation of the financial plan for each new year is much like making New Year's resolutions. Completion of the task evokes from many executives a sigh of relief and the resolve that "next year will be different." The problem experienced by many companies stems from difficulty with the sales forecast; often it is very late, resulting in a "crash" program to complete the financial plan on time—or if the forecast is on time, it proves to be inaccurate.

DIFFICULTY IN FORECASTING SALES

The difficulty in obtaining a more accurate and more timely sales forecast warrants a greater understanding of the problems before the sales department is criticized too severely. The difficulty stems to some extent from the increasingly important role being played by the government. The government sector plays a vital part in such projects as the space program, highway construction, mass transportation, water and air pollution, urban renewal, and defense. Because of voter sentiment, which is frequently conditioned by highly emotional issues, government spending is not as predictable as spending in the civilian sector of our economy. This causes uncertainty in the forecasting and time phasing of sales and results in problems when preparing a financial plan.

The financial plan for the coming year must be completed within a relatively short period of time—delays in receiving sales information notwithstanding. The answer is to develop cost information for the normal range of activity without waiting for the sales forecast. Then, when the sales become known, the projected costs for that level can be readily ascertained.

This approach, known as flexible or variable budgeting, has two basic advantages:

- It allows more time for formalization of the sales forecast.
- It provides the flexibility for adjusting budgets when there are changes in the sales plan during the year.

USING A FLEXIBLE BUDGET

Developing cost information for a range of volume—rather than for a single level—is specifically the reason the flexible (variable) budgeting technique was developed. Since it recognizes volume changes through the use of a variable allowance based on levels of activity, variable and fixed components of the budget formula can be developed well in advance of receipt of the sales forecast.

In most companies the new year's sales projection should not produce surprises. If during the year the sales department finds that a competitor has come out with a new version of a product, the information is acted on without waiting for an end-of-year projection for the new year. The required changes to facilities are known and implemented. Thus the basic cost information required to develop a flexible budget is available.

When the flexible budget formula has been completed for all departments and expenses, it should be tested through the development of a breakeven analysis. Developing the breakeven point on an overall basis is preferable to seeking department-by-department approval of the budget. The reason is that the breakeven point provides a comprehensive overview of the acceptability of the budget—eliminating time-consuming discussions and approvals which might be voided anyway if the breakeven point is too high.

The most difficult task in developing the flexible budget formula is the segregation of fixed and variable costs. Since there are several methods for accomplishing this, it might be well to discuss the advantages and disadvantages of each.

SEPARATING FIXED AND VARIABLE COSTS

The classic method, usually given "top billing" in textbooks, is the *scatter chart*. The principle followed in this method is to determine from historical data the relationship of expense to volume by plotting 12 to 15 months' data on graph paper. The vertical axis is used to represent the amount of expense, while the horizontal axis represents the level of activity. Each month's expense is plotted with reference to both scales. Theoretically, the points representing the expenses should show a linear pattern—sloping from zero (if the expense is completely variable) to some value representing the amount of expense at the highest volume level experienced during the period plotted. If the expense contains an element of fixed cost, the line will intersect the vertical axis above the zero point—that point representing fixed costs. The slope of the line will show the variable portion of the expense.

In theory, the scatter chart is a sound method for segregating fixed and variable costs. However, in the real world of business, costs don't behave with quite the amount of precision required to make this method effective. Most businesses are subject to fluctuating levels of activity. When a factory, for example, is preparing for an increase in volume, certain departments such as production scheduling, inventory control, purchasing, industrial engineering, and personnel are working at high volume—while factory activity is still low.

The production control group is busy analyzing schedules and the stockroom personnel checking inventories to determine what items must be ordered. The purchasing department is soliciting quotations from suppliers and placing orders. Some 8 to 10 (or more) weeks later, when the material has been received, the receiving personnel and stockroom employees will be busy storing the new material and preparing kits for issuance to the production lines.

Likewise, the personnel department is recalling employees from layoff, while the industrial engineers are laying out and balancing the production lines.

All of the forementioned departments are operating at a high level of activity and incurring overtime, while factory activity is relatively low. When everything has been readied and the volume of production rises, the service departments taper off in their activities. As a result of this counteraction between the service and production activities, the scatter chart becomes a hodgepodge of points which tell a very confusing story.

Those who are mathematically inclined will propose the *least squares formula* as the solution when the scatter chart is difficult to use. When the basic data defy analysis through simple scatter charting, it is not likely to show any clearer results when the points are fitted to a formula. In fact, the data may be even further distorted because of the tendency of the least squares formula to unduly weight extreme items.

With the advent of the computer, there are many who look to the magic of electronic technology to work out a mathematical model that will provide the breakout of fixed and variable costs. The *computer* approach has all the disadvantages of the scatter chart because it uses the same data. In addition, it uses techniques very similar to the least squares formula. The computer does not, at this time, provide the answer.

If a mathematical approach is to be followed, then the *low-high method* is superior to the three methods thus far discussed. In this procedure a certain amount of judgment is used in selecting two estimates of volume and expense within the normal range of activity. The use of this approach is demonstrated in four steps:

Step 1. Assume that you drive your car within a range of 1000 and 2000 miles per month.

Step 2. When you drive 1000 miles per month, assume that your monthly cost is $60. At a level of 2000 miles per month, let us suppose that this cost increases to $80.

Step 3. Putting the first two steps together, we arrive at the formula for ascertaining the variable cost per mile:

	Low	High	Difference
Miles per month	1000	2000	1000
Cost per month	$60	$80	$20

The variable cost is determined by dividing the variation in mileage into the variation in cost ($20 divided by 1000 miles). This gives us a variable cost of $0.02 per mile. The variable cost for the two levels, then, is:

Low	High
$20	$40

Step 4 The next step in arriving at the budget formula is the determination of the fixed cost per month. This is done by subtracting the variable costs shown in step 3 from total costs in step 2:

	Low	High
Total cost (step 2)	$60	$80
Less variable cost in step 3	20	40
Fixed cost	$40	$40

Using the Budget Formula to Budget Costs at Various Levels

Continuing with our example of the automobile, let us now budget cost for the operation of our car for several levels between 1000 and 2000 miles per month.

Number of Miles	Fixed Cost per Month	Variable Cost at $0.02 per Mile	Total Budget
1000	$40	$20	$60
1300	40	26	66
1600	40	32	72
1800	40	36	76
2000	40	40	80

A characteristic deficiency of all the methods discussed thus far is that the fixed cost is determined in a "lump." A department head given a budget formula for his department would be somewhat confused if he were told that his fixed expenses were "so many dollars per month" without knowing what was contained in this total. The next method, called the step method, overcomes this deficiency.

In the *step method* a budget is determined for each expense for various capacity levels—ranging, say, from 60 to 100% in increments of 5%. When activity in a particular month approaches one of these levels, the total budget for that capacity level is used. This method is quite sophisticated and requires that capacity levels be measurable. Measurability is not always possible when there is a multiplicity of diverse operations. Businesses considering the use of the step method should first assure themselves that they have fairly well-standardized manufacturing processes and acceptable denominators for measuring activity levels.

The method we prefer might be called the *participation* method. It consists of the identification of specific items of cost as to their fixed and variable characteristics. This identification and classification process is accomplished with the direct participation of the department head responsible for controlling the cost. Since indirect labor, with fringe benefits, may account for 65 to 85% of all overhead, this item warrants the use of an approach that is more analytical than graphs or mathematical formulas. If, therefore, a job-by-job analysis is made in determining the fixed and variable characteristics of each position, the semivariable factor can be ignored since it will automatically disappear. Once indirect labor is disposed of, several major cost items can be classified with relative ease. These are depreciation and occupancy costs, which are fixed, and maintenance of equipment, which is generally considered variable with the use of the equipment.

The foregoing expenses may account for as much as 85 to 90% of total overhead expense. The remaining 10 to 15%, which can be made up of from 30 to 50 items, can be dealt with on a fairly arbitrary basis—with little loss in overall accuracy but with a saving of valuable time.

This method of separating fixed and variable costs has the advantage that it requires the involvement of the department manager. By becoming involved, he becomes more interested in controlling his costs because he understands how they were budgeted, having been a party to the determination of the budget formula.

FORMALIZING THE FLEXIBLE BUDGET

Once the budget formula has been developed for the various expenses, the data should be formalized and presented in the form of a report which can be reviewed by key management personnel. This has two basic benefits:

1. It becomes an educational tool. Many key executives do not understand the intricacies of flexible budgeting and breakeven points. By reviewing a formalized report showing development of the flexible budget and the breakeven analysis, the executive can, in private, follow the steps and become familiar with the techniques.

2. The report provides the basis for reviewing the operations for cost savings. Some of the types of savings realized by several companies are described below.

SAVINGS RESULTING FROM REVIEW OF THE FLEXIBLE BUDGET REPORT

The general manager of one company, in reviewing the staffing of each department as shown in the development of the budget formula, noted that there were 11 sweepers in two adjacent departments. As a result of this observation, an automatic sweeper was purchased and 9 of the 11 sweepers were eliminated.

The plant manager of another company, who was accustomed to seeing only total salary and wage information without an individual job staffing breakdown, noted in his flexible budget that he had seven elevator operators. "Why," he asked himself, "in this day and age of automation, are we operating elevators manually?" As a result of this observation, automatic elevators were installed—with a payback within three years.

The executive vice president of another company, who also had previously seen only total wage and salary figures by department, noted in his flexible budget report that five maintenance craftsmen were assigned to a three-year project to overhaul equipment at a total cost of $165,000. Although this executive had been a party to the arrangement to undertake the project, his new overview prompted a question regarding the desirability of replacing the equipment rather than rebuilding it. He then raised a question as to the cost of new equipment and found that it would be $225,000—$60,000 more than the cost of rebuilding. However, because of the automatic features of the new machinery, direct labor costs would be reduced by $40,000 annually. On the basis of these facts, which were sparked because of availability of a job-by-job analysis in the budget, the overhaul program was discontinued and new equipment was purchased.

Preparing a budget logically and evaluating its contents in proper perspective can produce cost savings equal to if not greater than any of the savings achieved through comparing actual costs against the budget.

Cost techniques for planning, then, should have for their purpose not merely after-the-fact measurements; they should be designed to provide the professional manager of a business with the kind of overview of operations and a breakdown of cost elements in such a fashion that he can make sound decisions that will result in more profitable operations.

CHAPTER 8

ASSURING PROFITABILITY FOR NONSTANDARD PRODUCTS AND SERVICES

Unlike earlier case studies, this one, for a job costing operation, covers a broad spectrum. It starts with classification of expenses, reporting, and control by element of cost, relating these elements back to the estimate used to develop the price, and goes on to cash forecasting and profit projection. This chapter is "must" reading for anyone doing work for the government.

The normal conception of a business is that of continuous and repetitive operations in which there is a steady stream of standard products and services. This is not always the case, however. Many businesses provide products and services that are somewhat different one from another. Examples are a new type of jet engine or a different type of railroad train to fit in with high speed transportation requirements.

Although such products require a high degree of engineering combined with production, competition forces many companies to take such work on a fixed-price basis rather than the more appropriate "cost-plus."

Assuring profits for this type of nonstandard product is more difficult and requires a different approach than that normally taken for a conventional business. The recommended method is similar to that used by the construction industry in which each contract represents a different configuration which must be separately designed and individually estimated for pricing.

Since construction industry problems in assuring profitability are quite similar, this chapter discusses construction costing and cost control for profitability.

NATURE OF THE INDUSTRY

The construction industry includes numerous specialties. The contractors in the industry probably come closest to depicting the "rugged individualist" so well associated with the early growth of American industry. While ruggedness is an essential attribute, it implies a pragmatic approach to problems and a disdain for paperwork. Yet, because of the intense competition, the construction executive must intelligently plan his operations and assure himself that the plan is being followed. He must exercise control over labor, over the status of the various jobs, and over cash. Unfortunately, this means paperwork—the type and amount are the topics of the sections that follow.

FUNCTION OF THE CHART OF ACCOUNTS

In the course of a year, even a small company completes thousands upon thousands of financial transactions. These must be identified by category and then classified by account in order to facilitate meaningful reports which can be used by management.

A chart of accounts is the medium through which transactions are categorized and identified by account. General ledger control accounts are the major categories which, when formalized in statement form, provide the balance sheet and the income statement. Items within these categories are broken down further to provide more control.

While a contractor cannot be expected to know all of the intricacies relative to the books of account, he needs to be more familiar with the accounting flow of information than his counterpart in repetitive manufacturing. Unlike manufacturers, a large number of contractors are owners of their businesses. Because many of these businesses are relatively small, an owner cannot afford a highly skilled financial specialist on his staff. In many instances he hires an accountant to supervise routine activities, but must make the important financial decisions himself.

The contractor executive should be aware of the general flow of costs through the general ledger and should know that this ledger serves as a vehicle for preparing the financial statements—the balance sheet and the income statement. Although the balance sheet and the income statement are important overview statements, they do not provide the more specific types of control so necessary to assure profitability.

One of the basic tools for achieving more specific controls is a chart of accounts. A chart of accounts is the systematic organization and classification of accounts along with the assignment of numbers so that the sequential arrangement of numerical codes develops logical reporting formats. The accounting manual used by the Mechanical Contractors' Association of America includes such a chart in which the first three digits identify general ledger accounts through which balance sheet and income statement items are identified. Further coding beyond the first three digits provides information needed for more specific types of control. The use of the chart of accounts concept is demonstrated in the following discussion.

Balance Sheet

The 100 and 200 series are reserved for the balance sheet—the 100 series indicating assets, and the 200 series identifying liabilities and capital account. Each of the items shown in the listing below represents an individual page in the general ledger.

Total Assets (100 Series)
    102   Cash, Regular
    106   Cash, Payroll
    111   U.S. government securities
    121   Accounts receivable, Current
    122   Accounts receivable, Retention
    131   Jobs in process
    171   Land

174   Construction machinery
184   Construction machinery, Depreciation

Total Liabilities and Capital (200 Series)
203   Notes payable
211   Accounts payable, Trade
222   FICA tax withheld
244   Accrued wages
266   Mortgages payable
281   Capital

Income Statement

Here the 300 series represent billings; the 400 series and the 800 series represent costs:

Total billings (300 series)
302   Billings, Construction work
308   Billings, Service work

Total construction costs (400 series)
401   Direct labor
403   Material
405   Equipment
407   Subcontractors
411   Other job costs (overhead)

800   General and administrative costs

Once an executive realizes that each of the individual numbers in each series of accounts indicates a page in the general ledger, he can then more readily understand the purpose of the general ledger and the subsidiary ledgers which feed into the general ledger.

Coding for Control

The major elements of construction costs, which must also be identified by job location, are usually broken down into:

1. *Direct labor.* Labor that is directly involved in the construction process in putting material and equipment in place. Effective control of this element of cost provides the greatest potential for profitability.

2. *Material.* Materials used on the job are those items that lead to and connect with the various equipment items. The unit cost is generally small in relation to equipment; the contractor is usually able to obtain prices from pricing sheets and catalogs furnished by jobbers and wholesalers. While materials are purchased for each job, many of the items are such that excess purchases can frequently be used on other jobs.

3. *Equipment.* Equipment has a high unit price in relation to materials. Purchases are normally priced before each acquisition by consulting the manufacturer.

Although equipment represents a substantial amount of money in some types of construction, this element of construction cost requires the least amount of control, from a dollars-and-cents point of view. Control, from the point of view of scheduling delivery on the job site, is very important, however.

While the estimating of equipment requirements in a job estimate is fairly accurate, this cannot be said for materials. Any attempt to arrive at an exact figure for the material element could result in greater cost than any resultant saving through the added accuracy. Obviously, there are always some higher unit value materials for which greater estimating accuracy will pay off.

The material and equipment elements of cost should be identified separately. By segregating equipment as a separate element, management attention is directed to material—which requires the greater amount of attention. Through a comparison of actual material costs with the amount shown in the estimate, a determination can be made as to whether or not material costs are in line.

4. *Subcontracts.* The same principle applies to subcontracts as to equipment. Once a price has been negotiated, little can be controlled except for monitoring progress and the quality of the work.

5. *Other job costs (job overhead).* These represent "indirect" costs such as job supervision, on-site telephone expense, permits, job insurance, and protection service. Similar types of cost not identifiable

with any specific job are charged to the general and administrative category—sometimes referred to as general overhead.

The more such costs, specifically identifiable with a job, that are charged to the job—rather than to general overhead—the more accurate the job costs will be.

For purposes of facilitating controls, the five elements discussed above are coded in further detail. The degree of detail depends upon the needs of a particular company. An example of such detailed codes is shown in Table 8-1.

Table 8-1   Illustrative Codes

	General Ledger	Job Number	Trade	System	Type	Area
Direct labor	401	101	2	08		1
Material	403	101	2		01	
Equipment	405	101	2			
Subcontract	407	101	2		50	
Other direct job costs	410	101	—			

The first—and very important—level of coding after identifying the general ledger control number is job identification. Every contractor who has more than one job in progress at one time should identify costs by job number. Each job, as it progresses, should be compared with the estimate originally made for the job. As change orders are authorized, job costs should be compared with revised contract costs.

Levels of coding beyond the job number are presented as illustrations rather than specific formats to be rigidly followed. In certain types of small jobs, identification by trade may be sufficient since the trade or craft frequently identifies the system. In a large job, however, where a high rise building is involved, identification includes floor numbers and even the quadrants of each floor.

Once the construction executive understands the basic purpose for coding the major control categories and the applicable detail segments, he is ready to consider the steps in effecting controls.

CONTROLLING THE ELEMENTS OF COST

The measurement of cost effectiveness usually implies the existence of a "standard" against which the cost is measured. In job costing (construction or otherwise) a bid estimate represents that standard—as it would in manufacturing operations in which a custom product is made.

Because certain jobs may not be suited to the particular company's expertise, it should avoid them. All bidding should be done on a selective basis—concentrating on those jobs that have the greatest potential based on the bidder's experience and qualifications rather than "taking on all comers."

Importance of Good Estimating

No one would question the importance of accurate, fully detailed, and documented estimates as a prerequisite to profitability. However, the detail followed in estimating should not be carried to a fault, because the expense can be unrealistically high if the particular job is one that is not likely to allow a high profit. Material, as distinguished from equipment, is an example in which reasonable approximations must frequently suffice. The higher the unit cost of the material, the greater the degree of accuracy desired. But as the unit price decreases, more arbitrary measures can be introduced. On the whole, material costs should come to within plus or minus 5% of the bid estimate. If it is found in the course of the job that the percentage is being exceeded, an investigation should be made to determine the cause.

It is also important to treat each change order as if it were a new job—assuring that costs incurred because of the change order are correctly estimated and priced.

The Job Cost Card—Heart of the System

The job cost card provides a record of all construction costs—a separate card or ledger page being assigned to each job. Exhibit 8-1

Exhibit 8-1

JOB COST LEDGER

JOB NAME _____   JOB NO. ____101____

Date	Ref. Folio	Remarks	Total Costs	(401) Direct Labor	(403 Materials	(405) Equipment	(407) Sub-Contract	(410-499) Other Direct Job Costs
9/7	PR	Weekly Payroll	$10,000	$10,000				
9/14	PR	Weekly Payroll	9,500	9,500				
9/21	PR	Weekly Payroll	6,500	6,500				
9/28	PR	Weekly Payroll	9,000	9,000				
9/30	PJ	Purchase Journal	80,500		$23,000	$30,000	$22,000	$ 5,500
9/30	CD	Cash Disbursements	3,500		2,000			1,500
9/30	RJ	Recurring Journal	2,000					2,000
		Balance 9/30	121,000	35,000	25,000	30,000	22,000	9,000

illustrates the basic format. Company preferences for format vary. While some post each month individually and then add a cost-to-date cumulative total, others prefer a duplicate set of columns which show every entry made on a current and also on a cost-to-date basis.

As is noted, postings to jobs are made from the payroll, purchase journal, and other subsidiary ledgers. The purchase journal, shown in Exhibit 8-2, illustrates how the totals for the month for each element of cost are summarized by account number and by job number.

The *totals by account* are posted to the appropriate account in the general ledger. For example, $11,000 for materials is posted to the 403 account; $3,000 to the 503 (service department) account, and

SPECIMEN PURCHASE JOURNAL

Date	Ref Folio	Vendor	Total Amount Payable	MATERIALS Amount	MATERIALS Acct No.	MATERIALS Job No.	EQUIPMENT Amount	EQUIPMENT Acct No.	EQUIPMENT Job No.	SUBCONTRACT Amount	SUBCONTRACT Acct No.	SUBCONTRACT Job No.	OTHER DIRECT COSTS Amount	OTHER DIRECT COSTS Acct No.	OTHER DIRECT COSTS Job No.	GEN. & ADMIN. Amount	GEN. & ADMIN. Acct No.	GEN. LEDGER Amount	GEN. LEDGER Acct No.
		Totals Month of —	$50,000	$15,000			$ 5,000			$ 8,000			$ 4,000			$10,000		$ 8,000	
		Summary by Acct. No.		$11,000	403		$ 4,500	405		$ 8,000	407		$ 650	437		$ 3,000	838	$ 2,000	164
				3,000	503		500	505					400	441		500	842	1,500	168
				1,000	603		$ 5,000						350	461		400	846	1,000	203
				$15,000									500	498		200	849	500	206
													350	537		1,900	856	2,500	266
													550	566		500	862	500	271
													450	641		1,000	864	$ 8,000	
													350	672		500	868		
													400	698		300	873		
													$ 4,000			700	891		
																1,000	898		
																$10,000			
		Summary by Job No.		$ 4,500		101	$ 3,000		102	$ 4,000		101	$ 1,200		101				
				3,500		102	2,000		104	3,000		103	900		102				
				6,000		103	$ 5,000			1,000		104	1,000		103				
				1,000		104				$ 8,000			700		104				
				$15,000									200		105				
													$ 4,000						

Exhibit 8-2

100

$1,000 to the 603 (fabrication department) account. The 503 account represents service other than on-site construction, while the 603 represents fabrication normally done off-site.

The *totals by job number* are charged directly to the job cards.

At the end of each month, the total postings to the general ledger for each account (material, equipment, subcontract) should be exactly the same as the totals on all the job cards for these same items. This tie-in is demonstrated in Exhibit 8-3.

Monitoring Nonlabor Costs

It was pointed out in an earlier section that there is minimal need for job cost controls for items such as equipment and subcontract costs. The reason is that once a commitment has been made, little more can be done except to assure that delivery dates for equipment and performance schedules for subcontractors are met.

In the case of job overhead, all costs that can be directly identified with a job should be charged directly to that job. Examples are nonworking foremen, small tools, job supplies, truck expenses, permits, and cleanup. Certain costs normally associated with general and administrative expenses should be reviewed to determine their applicability to a job. Drafting, for example, can frequently be charged directly to a job. Telephone expense, when it is incurred at the site, is a job expense. Contractor executives, selling expenses, and office equipment rental, however, fall into the category of general and administrative expenses.

Monitoring Labor Costs

Although nonlabor-type costs must be controlled in some measure, the main focus must fall on direct labor. Many contractors correctly follow the philosophy that "if you control labor, you control the job." Control of labor requires the identification of time worked by each direct labor employee and the nature of the work performed. Since the time card is the medium for collecting such data, it is important

Exhibit 8-3

ILLUSTRATION OF TIE-IN OF JOB COSTS TO THE GENERAL LEDGER

AS OF _____

GENERAL LEDGER

Construction Costs: 400 Series	Account No.	Account Balances
Direct Labor	401	$194,000
Materials	403	160,000
Equipment	405	192,000
Subcontract	407	112,000
Other Direct Costs	410 - 499	40,000
Total Construction Costs To Date		$698,000

Service Department Costs: 500 Series	Account No.	Account Balances
Direct Labor	501	$ 3,600
Materials	503	3,500
Equipment	505	4,000
Subcontract	507	1,600
Sub totals		$ 12,700
Other Service Department Costs	510 - 599	3,500 *
Total Service Department Costs To Date		$ 16,200

JOB COST LEDGERS

	Total	Job No. 101	Job No. 102	Job No. 103	Completed Jobs
	$194,000	$ 35,000	$ 40,000	$ 19,000	$100,000
	160,000	25,000	30,000	15,000	90,000
	192,000	30,000	35,000	17,000	110,000
	112,000	22,000	25,000	10,000	55,000
	40,000	9,000	7,000	4,000	20,000
	$698,000	$121,000	$137,000	$ 65,000	$375,000

	Total	Job No. 215	Job No. 216	Job No. 217	Completed Jobs
	$ 3,600	$ 700	$ 500	$ 400	$ 2,000
	3,500	600	800	300	1,800
	4,000	900	700	200	2,200
	1,600	400	300	100	800
	$ 12,700	$ 2,600	$ 2,300	$ 1,000	$ 6,800

*Not posted to job cost ledgers. These costs are absorbed by use of an overhead rate applied to direct labor when determining billings.

that the time card provide for reporting the hours and the identification of the work performed. The time card can be an individual card used by each employee showing the jobs he worked on during the day and the hours spent on each job. Or, in the case of a small contractor, a single time sheet can be used to report the hours of all employees at a job site.

The Hershman Sheet Metal Works of New Jersey, Inc. uses such a form which is illustrated in Exhibit 8-4. The form provides a matrix in which the columns across the sheet indicate the job tasks on which work could be performed. Various lines provide for listing the employees who worked on the job and the number of hours worked at each task.

The reverse side provides for comments or questions which might be raised in connection with work to be done. Prepaid postage is also provided so that the time sheet can be folded over, sealed, and placed in a mailbox.

Ben Vitcov, of the Hershman Sheet Metal Works, states: "With this type of reporting, my supervisor is in an excellent position to quickly update himself with the general field progress."

Identification of Job Tasks

More often than not, the original estimate for a job does not show sufficient detail as to job tasks to be performed. Therefore, when a bid materializes into a firm contract, the estimator, together with the project manager, should break out the labor portion of the bid by job tasks or segments. As previously indicated, a small job (using mechanical contracting for illustrative purposes) might be broken down by plumbing and steamfitting. This automatically identifies two major systems that should in this case be reported individually. For a larger job the plumbing effort might be broken down into three segments:

1. Sanitary, Piping
2. Water, Potable
3. Setting of fixtures

For a still larger job, "sanitary, piping" might be shown:

Exhibit 8-4

DAILY OUTSIDE TIME SHEET

Red Fox
JOB Shopping Center ___ JOB NO. _____ 16 _____ TRAVEL TIME RATE $ 18.95 _____

THIS SHEET FILLED OUT BY ___ J. Jones _____ DATE March 9, 19xx _____

TODAY'S PROGRESS (DAY Friday)_____

___ Finish duct in food store. Install two 84 x 36 registers. _____

HOURS SPENT AND TYPE OF WORK DONE

NAME		S20 - DISTRIBUTE MATERIAL	S21 - ERECT DUCT	S22 - ERECT BREECHING	S23 - INSTALL CASING	S24 - ERECT FLUES	S25 - SET FANS & VENTS	S26 - SET GRILLES & DIFFUSERS	S27 - OTHER INSTALLATION	S28 - JOB SUPER	601 OUTSIDE SUPER						TOTAL MAN HRS.
H. Riker		6					2										8
R. Smith		6					2										8
E. Brown		6					2										8

TOTAL HOURS FOR DAY ▶ | 24

EXPENSES

SPENT BY	SPENT FOR	AMOUNT
SAVE RECEIPTS-GIVE TO DRIVER		

NOTE:

ONLY ONE SHEET PER DAY PER JOB IS TO BE SENT
IN, MADE OUT BY JOB LEADER OR FOREMAN.
   FILL OUT SEPARATE SHEET FOR EACH JOB WORKED
ON EACH DAY.
   I CERTIFY THAT THE ABOVE INFORMATION IS
CORRECT

_____
SIGNATURE

FOR OFFICE USE ONLY

DATE RECEIVED_____   DATE ENTERED_____

CHECKED BY_____   APPROVED BY_____

Exhibit 8-4 (*Continued*)

Comments or Questions

_____

_____

_____

_____

_____

_____

_____

_____

_____

_____

_____ FOLD LINE _____

_____ FOLD LINE _____

FIRST CLASS
Permit No. 463
Rahway, N.J.07065

BUSINESS REPLY MAIL
NO POSTAGE STAMP NECESSARY IF MAILED IN THE UNITED STATES

POSTAGE WILL BE PAID BY

**Hershman Sheet Metal Works
of New Jersey, Inc.**
827 Martin Street — P.O. Box 76
Rahway, New Jersey 07065

TIME CARD

Exhibit 8-5

JOB NAME _____

Work Code	Description	8 - 19		8 - 26		9 - 2	
		Man Hrs	Amount	Man Hrs	Amount	Man Hrs	Amount
02-1	Sanitary Mains—Outside Underground	20	$ 120	35	$ 210	70	$ 420
02-2	Sanitary Mains—Inside Underground	70	400	140	800	160	920
03-3	Sanitary Risers—Inside Aboveground	35	190	45	250	95	520
06-3	Domestic Water Risers—Inside Aboveground			20	100	50	270
12-3	Steam Mains—Inside Aboveground			15	80	65	350
30-0	Boilers						
53-0	Plumbing Equipment & Fixtures						
81-0	Excavation and Backfill	40	250	50	320	30	200
82-0	Testing, Start Up, Adjust, Balance						
83-0	Hangers, Supports			10	60	20	120
84-0	Anchors, Guides					3	20
89-0	Rigging						
91-0	Material Handling	7	45	6	35		
93-5	Variances—Rainstorm						
93-6	Variances—Premium Overtime					15	40
	TOTALS	172	$ 1,005	321	$ 1,855	508	$ 2,860
(1)	(2)		(3)		(4)		(5)

SUMMARY SHEET

JOB NO. 101

9 - 9		9 - 16		9 - 23		Total To Date		9 - 30		10 - 7	
Man Hrs	Amount	Man Hrs	Amount	Man Hrs	Amount	Man Hrs	Amount	Man Hrs	Amount	Man Hrs	Amount
60		35		30		250					
	$ 360		$ 210		$ 180		$ 1,500		$		$
150		120		30		670					
	870		700		160		3,850				
75		125		75		450					
	430		680		430		2,500				
60		55		55		240					
	330		300		300		1,300				
70		60		120		330					
	370		320		620		1,740				
20						140					
	130						900				
35		25		30		120					
	210		150		180		720				
5		4		5		17					
	30		25		35		110				
						13					
							80				
100						100					
	600						600				
75		45		65		200					
	180		110		170		500				
650		469		410		2530					
	$ 3,510		$ 2,495		$ 2,075		$13,800		$		$
(6)		(7)		(8)		(9)		(10)		(11)	

107

1. Underground
2. Above ground

For even more detailed information the underground segment could be shown:

1. East wing
2. West wing

The degree of detail used in identification of labor segments can vary from one job to another. There is no pat rule as to how the segments should be established. The overriding consideration should be that the segment be small enough to facilitate determination of percentage of completion. For example, the duration of a particular segment should be short in terms of weeks of work, making it possible to identify each such segment as:

0% completion—Not yet started
100% completion—Segment completed

The individuals performing the function of project management and/or field supervision should establish the 0 or 100% completion for each labor segment as of the period's cutoff date. It is best, in the interest of objectivity, if this is done without reference to any previously completed reports. With the percentage completion figures filled in, the reports should be forwarded to the accountant for completion. The form is illustrated in Exhibit 8-5.

Upon completion of this form, it should be returned to the supervisor for any remedial action that may be necessary. In addition to cost reductions accruing from corrective action, the report can be helpful in identifying items in the estimate that might be consistently too high (or too low). Future estimating will thus become more accurate.

It is not sufficient, however, to merely review what has happened. The actual happenings must be compared with what should have happened. This is where the weekly labor control report comes into play. The totals by work code are transferred from the weekly summary sheet to the weekly labor control (Exhibit 8-6). These totals are then compared with the amounts in the estimate—after adjust-

Exhibit 8-6

Labor Cost Control

JOB NAME_____ JOB NO. 101 PERIOD ENDED 9/23

Work Code	Description	Bid-Estimated Labor		Change Orders Thru No. 3 Amount	Estimated Total Amount	Est. % Compl.	Budgeted Amount Complete	Actual Labor To Date		Gain Or (Loss) To Date
		Man Hours	Amount					Man Hours	Amount	
02-1	Sanitary Mains—Outside Underground	350	$ 2,000	$ 300	$ 2,300	50	$ 1,150	250	$ 1,500	($ 350)
02-2	Sanitary Mains—Inside Underground	600	3,400	200	3,600	100	3,600	670	3,850	(250)
03-3	Sanitary Risers—Inside Aboveground	1600	9,200	300	9,500	30	2,850	450	2,500	350
06-3	Dom. Water Risers—Inside Aboveground	1050	6,000	200	6,200	25	1,550	240	1,300	250
12-3	Steam Mains—Inside Aboveground	900	5,100		5,100	40	2,040	330	1,740	300
30-0	Boilers	300	1,700		1,700	0	—			
53-0	Plumbing Equipment & Fixtures	400	2,200		2,200	0	—			
81-0	Excavation and Backfill	200	1,200	100	1,300	90	1,170	140	900	270
82-0	Testing, Start Up, Adjust, Balance	100	600		600	0	—			
83-0	Hangers, Supports	200	1,200	100	1,300	60	780	120	720	60
84-0	Anchors, Guides	100	600		600	20	120	17	110	10
89-0	Rigging	50	300		300	0	—			
91-0	Material Handling	50	300		300	20	60	13	80	(20)
93-5	Variances—Rainstorm (A)							100	600	(600)
93-6	Variances—Premium Overtime (B)							200	500	(500)
	TOTALS	5900	$33,800	$1,200	$35,000		$13,320	2,530	$13,800	($ 480)
(1)	(2)	(3)	(4)	(5)	(6)	(7)	(8)	(9)	(10)	(11)

(a) Caused cave in.
(b) Labor shortage.

ment for percentage completion. For example, work on sanitary mains—Outside Underground is estimated to be 50% complete [(East wing 100%, west wing 0%) ÷ 2]. This 50% is applied to the estimated total amount of $2300 to arrive at the budget of $1150. Since the actual cost to date is $1500, an excess cost of $350 has been incurred. This becomes the red flag to alert the contractor executive.

In making comparisons with a budget (usually the bid estimate), it must be remembered that performance measurements are more reliable when hours, rather than dollars, are used. It is possible, for example, that the hourly rates used in bidding may not have correctly anticipated a recent union settlement. Use of dollars eliminates this type of distortion.

While comparison with the bid dollar estimate is important, in order to account for the full variation, performance must be evaluated separately so that corrective steps can be taken when efficiency starts to slip.

Sometimes a large variation is caused by forces outside the control of the work force, such as an extended rainstorm which delays progress, or the incurrence of premium overtime to catch up. These should be identified separately. Separate identification avoids distortion of the historical figures which will be used as a guide in future bidding.

REVIEW OF JOB STATUS

The successful contractor executive can not be satisfied merely to monitor the various elements of cost—he must at regular intervals develop an overview of the status of each major job. This is necessary for two reasons:

1. Change orders are constantly being received as jobs progress. Their effect on the overall job status must be known.
2. The retainage withheld by the owner reduces the contractor's cash reserves. Accordingly, he must continually monitor the efficiency of his billing operation to assure that he does not underbill.

Change Orders

Exhibit 8–7 is used to record all requests for changes and claims affecting the nature, scope, and price of the contract. This report is a "log" of all such requests.

Exhibit 8-7

1

JOB NAME FARRAGUT BUILDING   JOB NO. 10   CHANGE ORDER STATUS

NO.	CUST. IDENT.	PROJ. IDENT.	CHANGE DESCRIPTION	REQUESTED BY	DATE	SUB-CONTRACTORS	DATE QUOTED	QUOTED AMOUNT	PROCEED BY	DATE	CUST. CHG. ORD. NO.	DATE	FINAL PRICE
1	GR-2	GR-3	ADDITIONAL WALL FIN RADIATION	ARCH.	10-2	Insulation	10-9	1,539.12	-	-	00-2	11-1	1,539.12
2	GR-6	GR-7	DELETE ELEVATOR PIT DRAIN TILE	ARCH.	11-7	-	12-10	(450.20)	ARCH.	12-15	00-4	-	(575.72)
3		PO-6	ADJUST OIL TANK VENT HEIGHTS	ENG.	12-2	-	12-5	320.75					Cancelled
4			CLAIM FOR ADDITIONAL PIPING	PK	1-7	Insulation	1-7	1,200.32					
5	GR-17		DELETE VALVE ACCESS DOORS	GC	1-9	-	1-15	(300.00)	-		00-9	5-17	1,113.20
6	GR-21	GR-9	CHANGE DUCTWORK IN STORAGE	ARCH.	1-17	Sheet Metal	2-2	556.60	-		00-5	2-7	556.60
7		PO-13	TEMPORARY SPRINKLER	ENG.	3-3	Sprinkler	3-4	675.10	ARCH.	3-5	00-6	3-10	568.70
8	00-30	CB-17	ADD SELF-CONTAINED A/C IN BOILER ROOM OFFICE	ARCH.	5-9	-	5-16	556.60	-		00-11	6-1	556.60

2

JOB NAME FARRAGUT BUILDING   JOB NO. 10   ESTIMATED COSTS AND CONTRACT VALUE STATUS

CHANGES	ESTIMATED COST DATA (EVEN DOLLARS)							CONTRACT VALUE DATA		REMARKS
	EQUIPMENT	MATERIAL	LABOR	SUB-CONTRACT	JOB EXPENSE	TOTAL COST	ACCUMULATED TOTAL	FINAL PRICE	REVISED TOTAL	
ORIGINAL	248,954	160,140	175,745	536,950	11,200	1,132,989	1,132,989	1,242,000.00	1,242,000.00	
1	177	275	450	370	-	1,272	1,134,261	1,539.12	1,243,539.12	
2	(300)	(287)	(288)	-	-	(575)	1,133,686	(575.72)	1,242,963.40	
5	-	-	-	-	-	(300)	1,133,386	(300.00)	1,242,663.40	
6	-	-	-	460	-	460	1,133,846	556.60	1,243,220.00	
7	-	-	-	470	-	470	1,134,316	568.70	1,243,788.70	
4	-	300	420	200	-	920	1,135,236	1,113.20	1,244,901.90	
8	320	50	90	-	-	460	1,135,696	556.60	1,245,458.50	
Pass to subcontract	(11,000)	-	-	11,000	-	-				Purchased 11/1

Any receipt of request for change that may in any way be a basis for requesting additional payments should be logged in the change order status. Even at the risk of a premature or incorrect entry, this policy of logging should be adhered to strictly.

Too often, when a change is requested, the work is done without proper steps being taken to calculate and agree upon the proper amount of billing. Sometimes the contractor concludes that the change does not cost him anymore because there is no increase in manpower, so he doesn't attempt to collect anything to cover the change request. The additional income, besides compensating the contractor for costly loss of momentum occasioned by changes, can sometimes add substantially to the profitability of a contract. If this were a $100,000 contract that yields only a $3,000 profit (many contractors make even less), a change similar to item 6 of the change order status, in which ductwork is altered, can bring in $557 in additional income—increasing the profit of $3,000 by more than 18%. Actually, in this case the work was done with no increase in work force over and above what would have prevailed had the change never been requested. The $557 does, effectively, represent additional incremental profit.

The practice of logging all changes assures that opportunities for such additional income are not overlooked.

USE OF THE CHANGE ORDER STATUS REPORT

An individual change order status report is used for each job. Although the contractor assigns numbers sequentially for his own identification purposes, he should also indicate the customer's number as well. While this may seem to fall in the category of clerical routine, it is important because the customer cares little about numbers assigned by others; he needs to know his own number in order to take required action.

It is also important to indicate by whom the request for change was made, the date of the request, and the customer's change order number and date. True, these are routine clerical functions—but they can save time and money if properly executed.

ESTIMATED COSTS AND CONTRACT VALUE STATUS

This form updates the basic figures on the original contract as authorization is received to proceed with each change. The first line, marked "original," shows the breakdown of the contract by elements of cost. As each change order is approved for price by the customer, it is posted to this report. Each element of cost is shown for the change order, as well as the price agreed upon. The total accumulated contract cost, as well as the total contract value, is shown after each change order to reflect the current status. This information plays an important part in evaluating the monthly job status, which is discussed next.

MONTHLY JOB STATUS REPORT

This is undoubtedly one of the most important control documents a contractor can have. The president of a very successful contracting company stated unequivocally, "If my office were to go on fire, the one file I would make sure to grab would be my monthly status reports."

The job status report, shown in Exhibit 8-8, is divided into three sections:

1. Upper section: Costs
2. Middle section: Contract value
3. Lower section: Statistics

Costs

The upper section of this exhibit concentrates on presenting cost information only. The first column indicates, by element, the costs incurred to date. These are taken from the job cost cards.

The center column adjusts the original cost estimate by the latest authorized change orders. These figures come directly from the

3

MONTHLY JOB STATUS REPORT

JOB NAME **Farragut Building**   JOB NO.   10   AS OF __

ITEM	Costs To Date	Original Cost Estimate (Incl. C.O's)	Present Forecast of Final Cost
Equipment	$ 216,515	238,151	232,400
Subcontract	516,733	549,450	543,250
Materials	141,232	160,478	160,500
Labor	165,410	176,417	182,000
Other Direct Job Costs	11,037	11,200	11,500
TOTALS	1,050,927	1,135,696	1,129,650

Net Amount Invoiced **$ 1,108,188.00**

CONTRACT VALUE

Original Amount	$ 1,242,000.00
Authorized Change Orders	3,458.50
Estimated Value—C.O's In Process	
Extras for Principal Customer	
Extras for Others	
Revised Contract Value	$ 1,245,458.50
Gross Amount Invoiced	$ 1,231,320.00 *

STATISTICS

Current Mark Up % On Cost	10.25%
Earned Gross Profit to Date	$ 107,741
Earned Gross Profit—Prior Period	70,300
Earned Gross Profit—Current Period	37,441
Unabsorbed Gross Profit	8,068
Amount Overbilled	72,652

* Gross	$ 1,231,320.00	
10%	123,132.00	
Net	$ 1,108,188.00	

Exhibit 8-8

114

estimated costs and contract value status report. Note that the total of $1,135,696 is carried directly to the job status report by element of cost. This figure represents the original estimated cost plus all change orders that have been approved.

The third column indicates the estimated costs required to complete the contract. These figures are determined by the following steps:

- Review the efficiency of labor as indicated by comparison of actual with budget. Project the amount of labor required to complete the job taking into account the variations that have occurred and possible corrective steps which will be implemented.
- Evaluate the effect of gains and losses in purchase of equipment and contract value of subcontractors. Indicate the estimated final cost of the contract for these items.

Contract Value

The purpose of this section is to show how the original estimate of the contract price has increased (or decreased). It shows the original value and the net amount of increases due to change orders that have been approved. This figure is taken from the contract value status report.

Statistics

This section responds to some important questions, the answers to which every contractor executive should be intensely interested in having. Some of the questions to which answers can be found in this section are:

1. What is the current percentage profit I can expect if I complete the contract on budget?
2. How much of this profit have I already earned in the work I have done to date?

3. What was my profit in the current period?
4. How much profit is left to cover the remaining work?
5. How efficient have I been in billing my cutomers?

The answers to the above questions can be found on the following lines in the statistical section:

1. *Current markup percent on cost.* This percentage is an important key indicator which can show whether the percentage profit is improving or deteriorating with the addition of change orders. The 10.25% is obtained by dividing the latest profit of $115,809 ($1,245,459 — $1,129,650) by the estimated final cost of $1,129,650.

2. *Earned gross profit to date.* The amount of the $115,809 profit recovered to date is determined by multiplying the costs to date by the current mark-up of 10.25% ($1,050,927 × 10.25%).

3. *Earned gross profit, Current period.* This is determined by subtracting the previous month's accumulated earned profit of $70,300 from the current month's accumulated earned profit of $107,741. The amount is $37,441.

4. *Unabsorbed gross profit.* The amount of profit left in the contract is calculated by subtracting the total accumulated earned profit to date ($107,741) from the total profit of $115,809. The amount of unabsorbed profit therefore is $8068.

5. *Amount over- and underbilled.* This figure is an indicator as to whether the contractor has been keeping up with his billings. The subject of over- and underbilling is an important one and is dealt with in greater detail in the section that follows.

MONITORING THE BILLINGS TO CUSTOMERS

Normally, in contracting it is customary for an owner (or government) to finance the work in the form of progress payments made to the contractor. The prime contractor in turn makes the same arrangements with his subcontractors. In furnishing the owner's representative with the breakdown of costs subject to progress payment, it is general practice to allocate disproportionately larger amounts to the earlier stages of the work in order to recover some of the retainage held by the owner as his assurance of satisfactory completion. This well-known practice of "loading" the earlier phases of the work is frequently referred to as overbilling.

Billing is Not an Exact Science

All invoices (requisitions), no matter how accurate they are presumed to be, are either overbilled or underbilled; it is hardly likely that any billing is exactly right. This becomes particularly obvious when one considers that there can be varying requirements on the parts of different owners for whom work is being done. Take a case in which the billing for the current month must be submitted by the tenth of the month in which payment is to be made. This requires estimating payroll payments and payments for materials and equipment—not to mention billings by the subcontractor. All customers are not consistent with respect to the basis for reimbursing equipment costs. Some pay only when the equipment has been installed. Others pay when proof has been furnished that the items are on the site, while still others pay when the items are in the contractor's yard and proof is presented that insurance coverage is satisfactorily arranged. These variations in requirements make it necessary to institute procedures that can sometimes be quite demanding in time and effort. The greater the number of variations, the greater the chance of erroneous billings.

Effect of Over- and Underbilling

Over- and underbilling can give rise to certain illusions which can be misleading and result in incorrect management decisions.

Overbilling, a situation in which actual billings made to the customer are greater than the total incurred costs plus profit thereon, can:

* Result in greater inflow of cash
* Give an impression that profits are better than they really are

- Cause contractors to overcommit themselves because of a feeling of confidence
- Result in overextension and failure

Underbilling, which is the result of actual billings falling short of total incurred costs plus profit thereon, can:

- Reduce cash
- Result in overpessimism and missing out on opportunities
- Seeking more financing than is actually needed
- Result in "buying" jobs.

Measurement of Over- and Underbilling

Although a condition of over- or underbilling can lead to incorrect conclusions if not properly interpreted, there is another condition, "flying blind," that could be even more harmful—that of not knowing whether a job is either over- or underbilled.

The determination of whether a company is over- or underbilled —and the degree to which either condition prevails—is a relatively simple calculation which was demonstrated earlier in connection with the monthly job status report. This calculation is:

Total gross billings to date		$1,231,320
Total incurred costs to date	$1,050,927	
Earned gross profit to date		
(10.25% × $1,050,927)	107,741	1,158,668
Amount overbilled		$ 72,652

Since the amount billed exceeds the costs incurred plus the markup of 10.25%, there is an overbilled position. Management is in a greater position of security with such knowledge because it not only knows whether it is over- or underbilled on this job—but because the amount is known. Since there is usually more than one major job in progress, it is well to provide this type of information on major contracts as a matter of routine. This has been demonstrated for a small contractor in Exhibit 8-9.

Exhibit 8-9

MONTHLY OVER OR UNDER-BILLED WORKSHEET

				JOB NUMBER					
Period Ended		Total	101	102	103	104	105	106	107
	Total Contract Amount	$990,000	$140,000	$ 60,000	$215,000	$135,000	$320,000	$ 80,000	$ 40,000
	Billings to Date	559,500	63,500	40,000	130,000	75,000	215,000	23,000	13,000
	Costs to Date	391,000	52,000	35,000	80,000	50,000	150,000	16,000	8,000
9/30	Markup % on Cost	57,640	12% 6,240	20% 7,000	15%12,000	17% 8,500	13%19,500	15% 2,400	25% 2,000
	Should Have Billed	448,640	58,240	42,000	92,000	58,500	169,500	18,400	10,000
	Over or (Under) Billed	110,860	5,260	(2,000)	38,000	16,500	45,500	4,600	3,000
	Billings to Date								
	Costs to Date								
10/31	Markup % on Costs								
	Should Have Billed								
	Over or (Under) Billed								
	Billings to Date								
	Costs to Date								
11/30	Markup % on Costs								
	Should Have Billed								
	Over or (Under) Billed								

Gauging the Effect of Over- and Underbilling on Cash

Measurement of over- and underbilling should not stop at this point. Since overbilling is offset by retentions by the owners, it would be well to determine the net effect, taking into account not only retentions by the customer but retentions held from subcontractors. This has been done in Exhibit 8-10.

This exhibit lists, by job, the over- and underbillings and retainage due to subcontractors. Overbillings plus retentions from subcontractors result in an increase in cash; this is shown in column 3. Column 4 shows the amount of retainage due from the customer; this reduces cash. Column 5 shows the net effect on cash after column 4 is deducted from column 3. Estimated time of completion of each of the jobs, shown in column 6, provides information as to approximately when retainages will be repaid and overbillings may revert to underbillings.

CASH FORECASTING

Although retentions and over- and underbillings can have a substantial effect on cash, the actual forecast of cash must be made within a

Exhibit 8-10 Effect of Overbillings and Retainage on Cash as of 9/30

Job Number	Over-billings ($)	Retainage Due to Subcon-tractors ($)	Total ($)	Less Retainage Due from Customer ($)	Net Effect on Cash ($)	Estimated Month of Completion
101	5,260	840	6,100	6,350	(250)	December
102 (Underbilling)	(2,000)	500	(1,500)	4,000	(5,500)	November
103	38,000	2,000	40,000	13,000	27,000	March
104	16,500	1,500	18,000	7,500	10,500	January
105	45,500	3,000	48,500	21,500	27,000	March
106	4,600	400	5,000	2,300	2,700	April
107	3,000	—	3,000	1,300	1,700	April
	110,860	8,240	119,100	55,950	63,150	
	(1)	(2)	(3)	(4)	(5)	(6)

somewhat narrower frame of reference. Cash forecasting can be done day by day, week by week, monthly, or quarterly. The frequency depends on the particular company and its needs. When cash is in short supply, the period for which the forecasting is done becomes shorter; when cash supplies become more abundant, the period becomes longer.

Sources of Data Used in Forecast

Collections from customers are determined in the early periods from outstanding receivables. For later periods it is necessary to evaluate the status of the various jobs in order to estimate collections. For disbursements, job status is again referred to for estimating completion dates; projections are required for starting dates of new jobs and their billing value; estimates are made of payrolls, payments to vendors, and debt payments. The net result of these projections is illustrated in Exhibit 8-11.

The desired ending cash forecast in January is sufficient for the needs. However, the balances in February and March fall short of estimated needs, which are $60,000 in February and $65,000 in March. Accordingly, additional financing of $41,600 is required in February and $81,600 in March.

Feedback Requirements

As in budgetary control procedures, feedback of actual results against the projections is very important. Such comparisons facilitate updating cash forecasts to take into account any changes in basic conditions which may have occurred. Feedback permits monitoring the effectiveness of cash management. Sometimes it is possible to defer payment of some invoices and to accelerate collections in order to meet an anticipated tightness in cash.

PROFIT PROJECTIONS

The monthly job status report serves not only to furnish information on the status of each major job—it provides the starting point for

Exhibit 8-11

QUARTERLY CASH FORECAST
BY MONTHS

	January	February	March
Beginning Cash Balance	$ 40,000	$ 62,100	$ 58,400
Estimated Cash Receipts			
Collections from customers	80,000	50,000	95,000
Collections from others.............................	5,000	2,000	6,000
Total Receipts.............................	85,000	52,000	101,000
Total Cash Available...........................	125,000	114,100	159,400
Estimated Cash Disbursements			
Net Payrolls	20,000	35,000	45,000
Payroll taxes & fringe benefits	2,400	2,800	4,000
Vendors..	18,000	29,000	37,000
Subcontractors	7,000	13,000	19,000
Income taxes	—	—	30,000
Other taxes.....................................	1,000	1,200	5,000
Insurance premiums..............................	3,000	—	8,000
Other expenses	8,000	11,200	13,000
Fixed asset purchases	—	—	5,000
Loans, notes, mortgage payments	3,500	3,500	10,000
Total Disbursements........................	62,900	95,700	176,000
Cash Excess or (Deficiency).............................	62,100	18,400	(16,600)
Estimated Financing Required	—	41,600	81,600
Ending Cash Balance................................	$ 62,100	$ 60,000	$ 65,000

projecting profits into the near-term future through the unabsorbed gross profit figure.

In the first month of the projection shown in Exhibit 8-12, the unabsorbed profit for each of the jobs is listed and totaled. This total is subtracted from the unabsorbed balance of the previous month to arrive at the amount of gross profit for the current month.

The amount of gross profit remaining for each job is then projected over each of the remaining months it will take to complete the work. As new jobs are started each month, the anticipated profit from these is included in the figures.

The current month's gross profit for each of the months can be compared with the projected General and administrative expenses to determine what the pretax profit will be.

Exhibit 8-12

MONTHLY GROSS PROFIT
PROJECTION SHEET

(1) Unabsorbed Gross Profit	9/30	10/31	11/30	12/31	1/31	2/28	3/31	4/30	5/31
JOB NO.									
101	$ 8,800	$ 7,500	$ 6,000	$ 3,500	$ 2,000				
102	15,000	11,000	9,000	8,000	6,500	$ 5,000			
103	32,000	28,000	24,000	20,000	17,000	12,000	$ 10,000		
104	18,000	14,000	9,000	6,000	5,000	3,500	2,000		
105	62,200	49,000	42,000	35,000	25,000	23,000	19,000		
106				25,000	20,000	17,000	15,000		
107				15,000	12,000	8,000	6,500		
108					7,500	5,000	3,500		
109					16,000	10,500	8,000		
110						65,000	56,000		
111									
112									
113									
114									
115									
Total Unabsorbed Gross Profit	$136,000	$109,500	$ 90,000	$112,500	$111,000	$149,000	$120,000		
Unabsorbed Balance—Prior Mo.	$157,000	$136,000	$109,500	$ 90,000	$112,500	$111,000	$149,000		
Add: Jobs Started This Month	—	—	—	40,000	23,500	65,000	—		
TOTAL	$157,000	$136,000	$109,500	$130,000	$136,000	$176,000	$149,000		
Less: Unabsorbed Balance This Month	136,000	109,500	90,000	112,500	111,000	149,000	120,000		
ABSORBED GROSS PROFIT	$ 21,000	$ 26,500	$ 19,500	$ 17,500	$ 25,000	$ 27,000	$ 29,000		

(1) Estimated gross profit remaining
to be realized on jobs in progress.
(From Monthly Job Status Reports—
See Exhibit 8-8)

As each month's results are available, the latest figures from the job status reports are posted to the projection sheets and adjustments made, as required, for the remaining months—thus providing a continuously updated profit planning tool.

ASSURING PROFITABLE OPERATIONS—SUMMING UP

The executive responsible for profitable operations in a nonstandard product or service is faced with a greater variety of problems than his counterpart who produces a standard product or service. Such an executive is required to be highly flexible and must "wear many hats." He is limited in the amount of detailed attention he can give to the various facets of the business. To assure that maximum emphasis is placed on cost effectiveness, these guidelines are recommended:

1.   Treat changes that are requested to the job as if they were new work. Each change should stand on its own as a profitable adjunct to the main contract.

2.   Identify the elements of labor in small enough segments to highlight a problem before it becomes a large loss.

3.   Identify the same elements in the original estimate to provide the means for monitoring costs against a budget. By comparing the actual hours and/or dollars with the original estimate, you not only measure cost effectiveness—you also measure the estimating accuracy.

4.   Identify and code separately unusual items so they do not distort historical costs.

5.   Know whether you are over- or underbilled. You should never be in an underbilled position at the beginning of a job.

Although the points covered in this chapter are directed toward the non-standard types of products and services, some of these can be employed in other industries. The profit-minded executive will remain continually alert to every possibility to improve profits. No industry has an "exclusive" on innovative ideas.

Note: Copies of the MCA Managerial Accounting and Cost Control Manual, from which some of the material was taken for this chapter, can be purchased from Mechanical Contractors Association of America, 5530 Wisconsin Avenue, N. W., Washington, D. C. 20015

CHAPTER 9

A COMMONSENSE APPROACH TO PROFIT IMPROVEMENT

Cost control methods applied to raw materials and direct labor can work well only if the men on the line—the supervisors—are aware of costs and the relative efficiency of their operations.

In a previous chapter we discussed the importance of a definitive plan with specific profit goals. We also noted that the effort required to formulate a good plan could point up important areas of cost savings through automation and simplification of product design.

Once realistic plans have been established, a flexible budget, covering the normal range of activity encompassed by that plan, should be developed.

The next logical step is the feedback of actual performance against the plan. The main thrust of this chapter is the improvement of efficiency with attention directed toward first-line supervisors, represented by the foremen of the producing departments and the managers of the service functions.

As a basis for discussion, it is helpful to first restate the parameters of the profit plan for the HiFi-Stereo Corporation, which was based on the following figures:

Investment	$3,375,000
Industry turns of investment in terms of sales	2½ turns per year
Required sales	8,437,500 ($3,375,000 × 2½ turns)
Industry profit on sales	10%
Industry return on investment	25% (10% × 2½ turns)

Our concern in this chapter is with the influence that first-line supervisors have on the improvement of return on investment.

THREE WAYS TO IMPROVE RETURN ON INVESTMENT

First-line supervisors can be instrumental in improving return on investment in three ways:

1. Reducing the amount of investment.
2. Increasing production volume without increasing the investment.
3. Reducing costs.

Let us consider these individually.

REDUCING THE INVESTMENT

Inventory in a manufacturing operation frequently represents a major portion of the investment. If the size of the inventory can be reduced and the number of turns per year increased, the return on investment will increase automatically.

Based on the figures in the HiFi-Stereo Corporation's profit plan, if the investment of $3,375,000 were reduced to $3,000,000 through a reduction in inventory, the return on investment would increase from 25 to 28% ($843,750 divided by $3,000,000).

Here are some ways in which the inventory can be reduced:

1. Establish good inventory records so the amounts of each item in stock can be readily ascertained. Effective inventory records require development of a good classification and coding system to avoid duplications.
2. Establish and maintain good methods of housekeeping and auditing. Proper housekeeping assures that an item can be found when needed. Proper auditing assures the accuracy of records. (A case in point: One company's division, which transferred its test equipment to another division, did not learn until after an audit six months later that $40,000 in electronic tubes for this equipment

was still being carried in its own stock. Meanwhile, the other division had purchased an equivalent new stock of such tubes.)

3. Standardize insofar as possible the component elements of product lines so the number of different items in the inventory can be reduced.

4. Shorten the manufacturing cycle by improved production techniques to speed the turnover of material. Schedule the delivery of major items needed for production as near as possible to the time they are actually needed.

While certain steps can be taken to reduce inventory, little can be done about reducing assets of a fixed nature—those represented by capital investment in land, buildings, and manufacturing equipment. (Of course, excess capacity in fixed assets can be sold either outright or through a lease-back arrangement, but that does not concern us here.)

In discussing the next step for improving the company's position, let us assume that sales volume (and therefore production) is increased 20% with no increase in investment.

INCREASING SALES VOLUME

With investment fixed at $3,375,000, assume that sales could be increased to $10,125,000. The resulting financial comparison would be:

	A	B
Sales	$8,437,500	$10,125,000
Profit (10%)	843,750	1,012,500
Investment	3,375,000	3,375,000
Return on investment	25%	30%
Investment turns	2½ times	3 times

Column A shows the same figures that were used in the profit plan. Column B shows how the return on investment would rise from 25 to 30% if sales increased from $8,437,500 to $10,125,000 without increasing the amount of investment.

The company's marketing department bears responsibility for increasing sales. Nevertheless, it is up to the first-line supervisor to promote the manufacturing efficiency that makes added sales possible. To do this he:

1. Minimizes downtime of equipment by a good program of preventive maintenance.
2. Sets methods for careful first piece checks to make sure equipment is not running bad production.
3. Groups and schedules those machines being operated by a single workman so that the workman can conveniently handle them all.
4. Schedules material flow between departments in such a way as to eliminate the downtime that results when one department must wait for a part from the department preceding it in the production cycle.
5. Provides adequate storage space so that tools not in use can be readily found when needed. Tools being returned to stock should be in good repair to permit them to be used promptly when needed.

REDUCING COSTS

Usually, the largest expense on an income statement is cost of sales. It is composed of three elements: material, direct labor, and overhead cost of the product.

These three elements vary in their proportions from company to company, depending on the nature of the product and the processes used for its manufacture. Typical differences are highlighted by the following tabulation.

	T	RT	Y
Material	80%	28%	59%
Direct labor	6	27	5
Overhead	14	45	36
Total cost	100%	100%	100%

Column T gives the breakdown for a manufacturer of radio and television sets. Here the material figure is high because many components of the product are purchased and then merely assembled. Obviously, this company should give primary attention to material in an effort to cut costs. Yet it is not unusual to find such companies devoting much more attention to monitoring direct labor, even though this element represents less than 10% of the value of the material in the product.

A company such as RT shows a more even distribution of cost elements. But the direct labor figure here runs far higher than for the other two companies. This suggests that RT might realize savings not only by efficiency controls but also by mechanizing to reduce labor cost.

Company Y illustrates a highly mechanized operation. By monitoring the productivity of machines and assuring that they operate at optimum levels, this company can maximize its efficiency and profits.

A cost breakdown similar to that shown tells the busy supervisor where he should start his economy efforts. If he starts with a major element of cost, rather than randomly, his chances of realizing substantial savings will be greater.

Let us review the three elements of cost—material, direct labor, and overhead—in more detail, with an eye to enhancing profits.

Material

Material is probably the most difficult cost element to account for. Many companies do not really know how much material they have used until they take a physical inventory, which is expensive and time-consuming. Because of the expense, most companies take inventories only periodically.

Yet, despite the problems in accounting for material use, the case for control is by no means hopeless. A small number of items usually makes up the bulk of the cost. Thus if a company is selective in taking inventories, it can do so more often—say, weekly—and thereby achieve a good measure of control, as demonstrated in the case of part no. 98986:

On factory floor	8,820
New issues from stock	69,000
Returns	(11,000)
Actually used	66,820
Should have used	24,066
Efficiency	36%

The listing shows that 8820 units were on the factory floor at the end of the previous week. For the current week's production, 69,000 units were newly issued from stock. Of this number, 11,000 were returned to stock because they were defective, not having been fabricated properly by another department. If we assume that at the end of the week's production no units were left on the factory floor, then 66,820 units were used. If we further assume that finished production for that week indicated that only 24,066 units should have been used, then the material efficiency for the item was 36%.

This low efficiency is due mainly to poor fabrication of part no. 98986 by another department, a deficiency that meant excessive use not only of parts but also of labor. Evidently, the plant was meeting a rush order which had to be satisfied and was too pressed for time to rework the defective parts to the standard they should have met in the first place.

For such information as we have given for part 98986, the first-line supervisor has a control report which spots trouble areas. Whether he is plagued by defective parts, poor workmanship of his own employees, or some other factor, he can tell from such reports where a greater degree of action is required.

Let us look at another listing, this one a report on a highly automated operation such as plastic molding. Here we consider the running hours of the machine and the pounds of material (in this example, powder) that were consumed.

Machine hours	7,343
Good units produced	13,705,000
Production should have been	14,761,094
Efficiency	93%
Powder actually used	221,690
Should have used	203,891
Efficiency	92%
Overall efficiency	86% (93% × 92%)

In most companies some variation of either this report or the one for part 98986 can be used as a signal to control costs of material. In general, the larger the share of the overall costs borne by material, the more sophisticated should be the methods for controlling this element of cost.

DIRECT LABOR

As automation increases under the competitive conditions of modern industry, the element of direct labor becomes smaller in relation to material and overhead. Direct labor is often found to be less than 10% of manufacturing cost. Still, for many companies, direct labor represents a major cost factor whose efficiency should be carefully monitored. This monitoring is usually accomplished through use of labor standards and labor productivity reports.

Although the purpose of labor standards is to provide a means for monitoring labor performance to assure greater productivity, the process of establishing standards and controlling performance is not as clear-cut as might be expected. There are two reasons for this:

1. It is not always possible to standardize labor operations to the point that every operation is measurable against a standard.
2. Continual changes in methods of manufacture and interruptions in production flow, attributable to circumstances outside the control of the labor force, negate the use of standards in the affected areas.

As a result, one frequently finds that although labor performance may be 90% or better for those operations that are on standard, the percentage represented by "standard" work may account for only half of the total work performed. The level of efficiency for the other half —if it is measurable against standards—might well be at an efficiency as low as 20%. Obviously, to report performance of labor while on standard and to ignore performance when not on standard can be misleading.

It becomes clear from this discussion that any measure made of direct labor cannot be localized within a narrow frame of reference —the big picture must be revealed. How this is done is illustrated with an example.

The standard for performing a particular job is assumed to be 20 units per hour. In a week, 7120 of these units were completed. The total earned hours was therefore 356 (7120 divided by 20). The actual number of hours required to complete these 7120 units was 383. The percentage of efficiency was 93% (356 earned hours divided by 383 actual hours)

However, in addition to the 383 hours shown above, an additional 320 hours were expended by the direct labor force in such tasks as material preparation, rework, and lost time because of poor material flow. When these 320 hours, which have been classified as indirect labor, are added to the 383 hours, the total reconstituted direct labor hours is 703. The revised efficiency percentage now becomes 51% (356 earned hours divided by 703). While it is helpful to the foreman to know that his direct labor, while on standard, performed at 93%, it is more important to know that on an overall basis the efficiency was only 51%.

While efficiency precentages can be an important indicator of performance, they do not equate performance with dollars. Without a knowledge of the dollars involved, it is entirely possible that much management time can be concentrated on improving the efficiency percentage of, say, 30%, which in terms of potential dollar savings might not be as significant as 40% in another department.

An alternative to complete reliance on percentages is a combination of percent performance while on standard and total labor cost per earned hour. With total labor cost expressed in terms of cost per earned hour, the foreman can compare this cost with what the standard cost should be per earned hour, as summarized in the tabulation.

	Performance While on Standard					Time on Standard (%)	Payroll Cost ($)	
	Earned Hours	Actual Hours	Per-formance (%)	Indirect Hours*	Total Actual Hours		Total Actual	Per Earned Hour
Standard	318	318	100	144	462	69	1656	5.21
Week end-ing 9/4	356	383	93	320	703	51	2973	8.36

* Breakdown normally shown on a supplementary report.

The steps in evaluating performance are:

1. Each succeeding week's results are compared with the standard shown above. The standard is based on a normal-sized crew working

a 40-hour week. Performance while on standard can reasonably be expected to attain 100% and even to exceed 100% with a bit of effort. The attainment of 356 earned hours was based on completion of good production amounting to this many earned hours but requiring some overtime. To attain this many earned hours required actual hours of 383, with the result that performance while on standard was 93% rather than an attainable 100%.

2. The standard shows that the labor force should have been on standard 69% of the time, but actual figures showed time on standard of only 51%. The excessive number of indirect hour charges was due to excessive rework and lost time because of delays in the flow of material. As a result, the actual payroll cost was substantially larger than it should have been.

3. To determine the trend of performance on a dollar denominator basis, the last column of the report shows the actual payroll cost per earned hour. This figure is $8.36 per earned hour as compared with a standard of $5.21. The excess cost is $3.15 per hour, which when multiplied by 356 earned hours to a total of $1121 in excess cost for the week.

SOURCE OF DATA

The preparation of such a report is contingent upon the availability of standards or estimates. This permits the determination of earned hours by extending total units produced by the standard or earned hours per unit.

Companies in which labor is an important element of cost should use standards and should prepare such a report at least for the major segments of the operation. It is unfortunate that some companies that use standards prepare highly detailed reports listing the performance by employee for each day and for each operation without ever focusing on the larger picture that highlights trends and provides a more actionable basis for making management decisions.

A report of the type described above provides first-line supervision with a realistic tool for control in a format that highlights trends. However, no report can achieve control in and by itself. A report can only report performance and highlight poor areas—the foreman must take the corrective action.

OVERHEAD

Overhead is usually that element of the manufacturing cost that cannot be directly identified by analyzing individual products. It consists of such items as:

Indirect labor costs
    Manufacturing superintendent
    Foremen
    Clerks
    Material handlers
    Maintenance men
Payroll-related expenses
    Social security
    Unemployment insurance
    Hospitalization
Indirect material
    Machine repair parts
    Chemicals
    Small tools
Purchased services
    Utilities
    Dues and subscriptions
    Guard services
Fixed charges
    Depreciation
    Real estate taxes
    Fire insurance

We have listed only a few items as examples; in most companies the list is much larger. In any event the question is: With so many different items to consider, how can we monitor overhead costs?

At the outset, we lay down two guidelines:

1. Certain costs vary with the level of production activity measured by such indicators as direct labor hours, machine hours, and the like.

2. Certain other costs remain more or less fixed within a normal range of production activity.

An example of variable costs is packing supplies. These usually are used up in direct proportion to the use of production equipment. To assign an allowance for packing supplies, we first consider their usage over a given period of time, adjusting the figure to eliminate any unusual, nonrepresentative elements. Then this figure is converted to a factor of so much per machine hour or so much per labor hour. This gives the foreman a yardstick for monitoring one aspect of overhead.

An example of fixed costs is depreciation or real estate taxes. These remain fairly constant, regardless of the volume of production activity. They are generally expressed as so much per month and assigned accordingly to the manufacturing cost.

In some instances, an overhead cost is neither wholly variable nor wholly fixed, but rather a mixture of the two. Indirect labor often comes under this category. The problem in such cases is how to segregate the variable from the fixed.

To illustrate, let us use this example of one company's material control department. Its makeup is as follows.

Manager	1
Secretary	1
Stock handlers	8
Schedulers	5
Total	15
Payroll per month	$8,000
Activity level per month (direct labor hours)	300,000

Suppose the department manager wants to know what the allowable payroll cost should be for an activity level of 275,000 direct labor hours, or 325,000. Once he identifies the variable cost portions in this department, he can adjust these to the appropriate level and add the fixed costs to arrive at a total allowable cost.

We can assume that the manager is a fixed cost, since he remains regardless of fluctuations in production volume. The same is true of the secretary.

As for the stock handlers, we must first know the nature of their jobs. One stock handler is stationed full-time at the receiving dock where he receives material, confirms quantities, and records the receipt. A second stock handler is permanently assigned to a controlled stockroom where he dispenses supplies, tools, and the like. A third stock handler is responsible for the movement of semiprocessed material from one factory work area to another. Because the jobs performed by all three are required regardless of fluctuations in production, they represent fixed costs.

We may consider the remaining five stock handlers variable costs because their work fluctuates with the volume of material to be moved, and this in turn is governed by the level of production activity.

When evaluating the schedulers, we find that three of them are each assigned full-time to a production line group. The remaining two assist where there is an overload in any of the groups. Thus three may be considered fixed costs and two variable.

The breakdown for the department may be calculated as follows.

	Total	Fixed	Variable
Manager	1	1	0
Secretary	1	1	0
Stock handlers	8	3	5
Schedulers	5	2	3
Total	15	7	8
Payroll	$8000	$5000	$3000

We see that the variable costs are $3000 for an activity level of 300,000 direct labor hours, or $0.01 per direct labor hour. Therefore, at the 275,000-direct-labor-hour level, the variable cost allowance is $2750; at the 325,000 level it is $3250. The fixed cost allowance remains at $5000.

The payroll allowance for the different activity levels is summarized as follows.

Activity Level (direct labor hours)	Total payroll ($)	Fixed ($)	Variable ($)
300,000	8000	5000	3000
275,000	7750	5000	2750
325,000	8250	5000	3250

Techniques such as described help to determine overhead allowances and thus to control costs. But it must be borne in mind that fluctuations in production activity cannot always be matched by changes in variable costs. That is because a temporary reduction in volume may not justify laying off personnel who may have to be rehired a month or two later. Meanwhile, the excess cost of retaining such personnel can be equated with the cost of building extra inventory during the low periods of production.

CONCLUSION

The mere existence of a good accounting system does not guarantee that first-line supervisors will have the control information they need.

In most companies the primary purpose of the accounting system is to present summary data to the owners or stockholders. Moreover, the form in which these data are gathered and presented does not readily lend itself to use by first-line supervisors, nor does it come with the frequency their needs require.

It is necessary, therefore, to develop subsidiary reporting procedures to assist lower-level management.

This procedure should aim at providing information that is timely and that concentrates on a few major items, not attempting to cover a broad spectrum.

A common sense approach to profit improvement can be summarized in five points:

1. Report significant data.
2. Include in these data only items that the first-line supervisor can control.
3. Compare actual costs with attainable standards.
4. Be alert to developments in trends.
5. Keep reports simple.

CHAPTER 10

EVALUATING PROFIT OPPORTUNITIES IN A NEW BUSINESS VENTURE

Assuring profitable operations in a going business frequently requires only modification of existing procedures. A new venture, however, must be evaluated from ground up—there are no existing procedures to modify.

Of the great numbers of persons who go into business, only a small number, estimated by various economists at from 10 to 20% meet with sufficient success to enable them to remain in business, while the remainder fail in their attempts. This points up the importance of making a careful appraisal of potential problem areas before launching a new business venture. It is the purpose of this chapter to demonstrate the approach to making such an appraisal. The business selected for study is subscription television—frequently referred to as pay TV. The choice of this type of business should be appropriate because we deal with a type of business that is relatively new and one whose problems should be fairly easy to visualize and understand.

Our investigations concern themselves with the selection of indicators that measure market potential and the characteristics of this market, while the second part of the chapter addresses itself to the determination of profit opportunities and capital requirements.

DETERMINING MARKET POTENTIAL

Probably the most important indicator of the market potential of subscribers in an area is an analysis of income stratification. Income by itself, while an important indicator, is not sufficiently comprehensive. It is therefore necessary to take into account such other indicators as education, occupation, age of the potential viewing audience, and family makeup.

Income Stratification

The median (or most frequently occurring) annual income in the area selected for study is $8300 per year—compared with $6235 five years previously. The increase over the five-year period represents a larger percentage than the corresponding increase shown by the national average. This is due to an influx of business and professional people attracted by several new residential areas. The breakdown for five income ranges is shown in Table 10-1.

Table 10-1   Breakdown of Income

Income Range	This Year (%)	Five Years Ago (%)
Under $3,000	1.2	3.7
$ 3,001 to $ 6,000	19.8	26.3
$ 6,001 to $10,000	62.0	58.8
$10,001 to $20,000	13.3	10.0
Over $20,000	3.7	1.2
	100.0	100.0

It is evident from the above that the first two ranges—under $3000 and between $3001 and $6000—have decreased, while the higher ranges of income have increased. Since the shift into the higher ranges is in excess of current inflationary increases, it can be concluded that the residents of this area are increasing their affluency at a greater rate than the nation as a whole.

Educational Profile

The educational profile was based on a survey of the breadwinners of each household. The median level of scholastic attainment falls

Table 10-2   Educational Profile

Scholastic Level	Percent
No high school	4.5
Some high school	20.1
High school graduate	36.4
Some college	17.5
Undergraduate degree	16.6
Graduate work	4.9
	100.0

in the high school graduate category. Percentages of breadwinners falling in the various categories are shown in Table 10-2.

This analysis shows a fairly high educational level in the area being surveyed. The high level correlates with the relatively high income level—both important factors in the marketability of subscription TV. The educational level is a factor in determining the types of programs that would be in demand. The occupational breakdown is also important and is therefore considered next.

Occupational Specialties

Table 10-3 indicates that more than half of the heads of households fall in the executive and professional category—obviously an important indicator of viewer preferences.

Table 10-3   Occupational Breakdown

Occupational Category	Percent
Executive and junior executive	29.6
Professional	22.3
Skilled labor	16.5
White collar	10.6
Salesmen or owners of own business	10.4
Service	6.1
Retired	4.5
	100.0

Tastes and interests in programming are also influenced by age, by family makeup, and by the number and age of children in a household. These are dealt with next.

Age of the Breadwinner

The median age of the head of the household was found to be 43 years and 5 months (Table 10-4).

Table 10-4   Age Grouping

Age (years)	Percent
Below 20	0.6
Between 20 and 29	12.3
Between 30 and 39	26.4
Between 40 and 49	35.2
Between 50 and 59	12.1
Over 60	13.4
	100.0

The age profile of the breadwinner usually reflects the age level of the balance of the family, but it cannot be used in isolation. Marital status and number of children must also be used to temper the analysis.

Marital Status

A test of the area of study showed a significantly high number of married householders, with 84.7% living with their mates, 6.4% widowed, and 8.9% single or living separately from their mates.

Children

The average number of children found per household in this survey was 2.2. More than half of the households had two children. The

Table 10-5   Age Breakdown of Children

Age of Children	Percent
Kindergarten age and below	24.6
6 through 10 years	23.5
11 through 15 years	21.6
16 through 20 years	22.3
21 years and over	8.0
	100.0

average age of the children was found to be 12, the distribution of which is shown in Table 10-5.

Because the average age of the children in this area is greater than in one of the nearby areas with subscriber TV (12 versus 10.9 years), programming for children will most likely be affected by this average age difference.

Tempering the Statistics with Judgment

Evaluation of the potential profitability of a venture can not be determined by cold statistics alone. As in any business endeavor, judgment must be brought into play. Consideration must be given to the factors that motivate people to become subscribers.

- Is it newspaper ads, high pressure door-to-door salesmen, or the expectation that program content will be superior to conventional television?
- However, it is equally important to know why subscribers drop out. The reasons for disenchantment on the part of these "dropouts" could present problems to any other similar venture.
- Was the problem due to inability to obtain enough good films? If so, investigation is needed to determine if this will be a problem for the proposed new venture.
- Are so-called "good films" so loaded with sex and violence that subscribers would not want them in their homes for fear that their offspring will be exposed to them?
- Is the potential subscriber becoming disenchanted with all types

of home entertainment—in favor of seeking amusements outside the home? The pendulum for tastes has a tendency to swing from one extreme to the other. If a reversal in the cycle is due, then additional resistance must be overcome—and this must be recognized.

While the answers to these questions require a probing analysis not readily available from cold statistics, a good deal of light can be thrown on customer preferences through questionnaires which have been carefully prepared to extract from them their preferences for programs and their willingness to pay for them.

Survey of Programs Watched

One such survey was made by obtaining information from a neighboring pay TV area through questionnaires mailed to subscribers in that area (Table 10-6). The operators of the system agreed to furnish

Table 10-6   Survey of Types of Programs Watched in a Neighboring Area

Type of Program	Percent
Film	44.2
Sports event	35.3
Children's film (cartoon types)	10.6
Night club acts	8.1
Broadway stage plays	1.8
	100.0

the names and addresses of their subscribers because they were also interested in the results, which would be made known to them.
The high percentage of time spent watching sports events was unexpected. Another unexpected finding (not shown in Table 10-6) was that almost half the films watched were of the B type, as distinguished from first-rate. This indicated that interruption of films by commercials might be an important feature upon which to capitalize in the advertising.

In making evaluations of this type, it must be remembered that programs watched are a function of programs that are available. Availability, to some extent, can affect viewing.

The results of a survey of viewers in an existing subscription TV area are likely to be more reliable than one conducted among prospects who have never experienced this type of programming. Nonetheless, the more information that can be gathered about the prospective subscribers, the better. The process of questioning serves an important ancillary purpose—advertising and developing interest in the new venture.

The questionnaires must naturally be carefully prepared to assure that questions arising from the previous survey are answered. The questions covered should include an expression of preference for various types of programs, requesting specific examples of the types of movies, stage plays, sporting events, and other types of entertainment desired.

Willingness to pay certain amounts for the various types of programs should also be ascertained, as should be the attitude toward installation charges of various amounts.

Once we are satisfied that viewer preferences are known, and the schedule of fees has been determined, we are ready to summarize data relating to the total potential market.

The Potential Market

The area selected for the new venture covers about 28 square miles and is located about 30 miles from a major city which transmits programs from three channels. Because of the surrounding hills, only about half of the residents in the area receive all three channels. The other half receive two channels with varying degrees of quality.

Interest in receiving better reception and more programs is high. This is reflected by the fact that there are more than 2700 TV homes per square mile—a total of 75,600 for the selected area (2,700 per square mile $\times$ 28 square miles).

Sampling surveys (both by telephone and by mail) made of these 75,600 TV homes showed that 47.5% expressed interest in becoming subscribers. This compared with an actual percentage of installations in the neighboring area of 42%—in spite of a lower density of TV homes amounting to only 2300 per square mile.

Applying the 47.5% to the total TV homes in the area showed a potential of 35,910 subscribers. In evaluating the time requirements for completing approximately 36,000 hookups, it was estimated that an average of slightly more than 3.5 subscribers could be tied into the system per workday. This includes stringing a cable as well as making the actual hookup to the subscriber's TV set.

This estimate allows for delays due to the more difficult terrain through which the telephone company would have to install additional poles leading from the transmitting unit on top of one of the hills. It also takes into account that construction of certain new residential areas is not to be started for at least another year.

With the number of subscribers and the time-phasing of the hook-ups established, the next step is to project the revenues and to match them against costs of programming, rental of telephone company facilities, start-up, operating, subscriber units, and transmission center equipment. These are covered in the second section of the chapter.

PROFITABILITY AND FINANCIAL REQUIREMENTS

This section deals with the projection of income, expenses, and capital requirements based on equity financing.

Income from Subscribers

The charge per subscriber has been estimated to average $15 per month or $180 per year. Since the amount of revenue is contingent upon viewing, the projection of each month's receipts must be adjusted by a seasonal viewing index which takes into account the changing interests of subscribers during the various months of the year. The index by months and its effect on monthly receipts is shown in Table 10-7.

Table 10-7   Breakdown of Subscriber Income by Months

Month	Viewing Index	Monthly Income per Subscriber ($)
January	1.2	18.00
February	1.1	16.50
March	1.1	16.50
April	1.1	16.50
May	0.9	13.50
June	0.9	13.50
July	0.8	12.00
August	0.8	12.00
September	0.9	13.50
October	1.0	15.00
November	1.1	16.50
December	1.1	16.50
		180.00

Income from Installation Charges

Field surveys indicated that subscribers were willing to pay an installation charge of $16. These were taken into income over a four-year period.

Expenses

Expenses are categorized as follows.

- Programming
- Rental of telephone company facilities
- Depreciation
- General and administrative expenses

Programming

This item required some analysis of industry experience. A check made with several subscriber television systems in other areas revealed that their programming costs averaged 41% of revenues. Revenues averaged $161 per year, or $19 per year less than was being planned for the new venture. This meant that the percentage of programming cost on a base of $180 would actually be 37%. Since it was planned to keep programming at a high quality level with additional emphasis on championship sporting events, the decision was made to allot 40% of revenues for programming costs.

Rental of Telephone Company Facilities

Arrangements with the telephone company provide that it will furnish a transmission cable, run it over telephone poles, and make hookups to the subscribers' sets. The cost for providing the cable and maintaining service will be $2,550,000 payable according to the following schedule.

Start-up period	$510,000
Six months after start	510,000
Annually thereafter until completion	510,000

For purposes of projecting the operating results, rental of telephone facilities, including hookups, was estimated at $1 per month per subscriber.

Depreciation and Amortization

Costs covered in the depreciation expense and the period over which taken are shown in Table 10-8.

Table 10-8 Depreciation and Amortization

	Total cost ($)	Years
Transmission cable	2,550,000	10
Hookups	2,048,000	4
Transmission center equipment	680,000	10
Hookup units	6,604,000	10
	11,882,000	

For operating statement purposes depreciation was based on the straight-line method.

General and Administrative Expenses

This item includes promotional expenses, engineering, administration, and costs associated with making collections.

Promotional Expenses

The sales manager, his salesmen, automobile rental costs, publicity material, and "On the Cable" (a TV program booklet) are included in this category of expense. The breakdown of these costs is shown Table 10-9.

Table 10-9   Promotional Expenses

	First year ($)	Start-up Cost ($)
Sales manager	20,000	10,000
18 salesmen ($9000 each)	162,000	40,500
Automobile expense	37,600	9,400
Payroll-related costs	25,500	7,100
Publicity material	3,600	98,000
"On the Cable"	1,200	600
	249,900	165,600

In the third quarter of the fourth year, the number of salesmen would drop to seven, since the saturation point would have been reached. The sales effort would then be concentrated on replacing subscribers lost through turnover.

Engineering

These expenses are related to the operation of the transmission center. They are listed in Table 10-10.

Table 10-10 Transmission Center Staffing

	First Year ($)	Start-up Cost ($)
Chief engineer	17,000	8,500
Two studio engineers ($14,250 each)	28,500	9,500
Four projectionists and cameramen	34,000	8,500
Maintenance technician	8,000	2,000
Two electronic maintenance men	15,000	3,800
Payroll-related expenses	14,350	4,500
	116,850	36,800

Although two electronic maintenance men are included in the annual cost, this represents the first year only. As installations increase, three more will be added at the start of the second year, three at the start of the third year, and two at the start of the fourth year. As the facilities become older, it may be necessary to add one additional maintenance man.

Automobile expense for the electronic maintenance men runs about 26½% of salaries paid. This is the guide used for projecting this expense. Such items as video and audio tape and replacement parts were projected on the basis of $1000 the first year, $2000 the second, $3000 the third, and $4000 the fourth. A summary of non-labor expenses for the first year and for the start-up period is shown in Table 10-11.

Table 10-11 Transmission Center Expenses

	First Year ($)	Start-up Cost ($)
Automobile expense	4000	1000
Tapes and replacement parts	1000	500
Supplies	200	100
	5200	1600

Administration

The office building and personnel performing administrative service are to be located in town rather than at the transmission center. In addition to the general manager, program director, and accounting personnel, the collection function will also be housed at the same location. Although the administrative costs, other than collections, will be fairly stable during the four-year period, the number of routemen responsible for making the collections will increase as the number of subscribers grows, using the ratio of one collector for 3000 subscribers (coin boxes will be emptied every two months). Automobile expense was projected to be 25% of the salary cost of the routemen. The listing of payroll and nonpayroll expenses is shown in Table 10-12 for the first year and for the start-up period.

Table 10-12   Administrative Cost Breakdown

	First Year ($)	Start-up Cost ($)
General manager	25,000	18,750
Program director	20,000	15,000
Two secretaries	12,000	6,000
Chief accountant	12,000	9,000
Switchboard operator	6,000	3,000
Bookkeeper	8,000	2,000
Four accounting clerks	24,000	6,000
Service bureau charges	122,000	
Payroll-related expenses	15,000	8,400
Sundry administrative expenses	65,000	32,500
Route manager	12,000	
Three route men	24,000	
Automobile expense	6,000	
Payroll-related expenses	5,100	
	356,100	100,650

The service bureau will supply weekly reports showing the number of subscribers viewing each program. These reports will also show the time the program is viewed and the revenue by program and by subscriber. In addition to the viewing statistics, this information will provide an audit check of collections.

Projected Income and Cash Flow

The income, expenses, and cash flow were projected by quarters over the four-year period it would take to complete the installations. Each of the four years is shown in Exhibits 10-1 through 10-4.

Exhibit 10-1   Projection of Income and Cash Flow

	First year				
	First Quarter	Second Quarter	Third Quarter	Fourth Quarter	Total Year
Number of subscribers	2,244	4,488	6,732	8,976	8,976
Income					
From subscribers	$ 75,200	$ 160,400	$ 231,100	$ 396,100	$ 862,800
From installations	1,700	3,800	6,000	8,200	19,700
Total income	$ 76,900	$ 164,200	$ 237,100	$ 404,300	$ 882,500
Expenses					
Programming	$ 30,100	$ 64,200	$ 92,400	$ 158,400	$ 345,100
Rental, Telephone company facilities	4,500	11,200	18,000	24,700	58,400
	34,600	75,400	110,400	183,100	403,500
Depreciation					
Transmission cable	2,700	6,700	10,800	14,800	35,000
Hookups	5,400	13,500	21,500	29,600	70,000
Hookup units	6,800	17,200	27,500	37,800	89,300
Transmission center equipment	17,000	17,000	17,000	17,000	68,000
	31,900	54,400	76,800	99,200	262,300
General and administrative					
Promotional expenses	62,500	62,500	62,400	62,500	249,900
Engineering	30,500	30,500	30,500	30,500	122,000
Administration	89,000	89,000	89,100	89,000	356,100
	182,000	182,000	182,000	182,000	728,000
Total expenses	$ 248,500	311,800	369,200	464,300	1,393,800
Pretax profit (loss)	($ 171,600)	($ 147,600)	($ 132,100)	($ 60,000)	($ 511,300)
Provision for federal and state taxes					
Net profit or (loss)	($ 171,600)	($ 147,600)	($ 132,100)	($ 60,000)	($ 511,300)
Cash flow					
Net profit or (loss) from above	(171,600)	(147,600)	(132,100)	(60,000)	(511,300)
Add:					
Provision for tax					
Depreciation	31,900	54,400	76,800	99,200	262,300
Deferred receipts from installations	34,200	32,200	29,900	27,700	124,000
Cash flow	($ 105,500)	($ 61,000)	($ 25,400)	$ 66,900	($ 125,000)

Exhibit 10-2　Projection of Income and Cash Flow

	First Quarter	Second Quarter	Third Quarter	Fourth Quarter	Total Year
			Second year		
Number of subscribers	11,220	13,464	15,708	17,952	17,952
Income					
From subscribers	$ 532,900	$ 550,900	$ 576,800	$ 826,900	$2,487,500
From installations	10,500	12,700	14,900	17,200	55,300
Total income	$ 543,400	$ 563,600	$ 591,700	$ 844,100	$2,542,800
Expenses					
Programming	$ 213,200	$ 220,300	$ 230,700	$ 330,800	$ 995,000
Rental, Telephone company facilities	31,400	38,200	44,800	51,600	166,000
	244,600	258,500	275,500	382,400	1,161,000
Depreciation					
Transmission cable	18,900	22,900	26,900	30,900	99,600
Hookups	37,600	45,700	53,900	62,100	199,300
Hookup units	48,100	58,400	68,700	78,900	254,100
Transmission center equipment	17,000	17,000	17,000	17,000	68,000
	121,600	144,000	166,500	188,900	621,000
General and administrative					
Promotional expenses	62,500	62,500	62,500	62,400	249,900
Engineering	38,600	38,700	38,700	38,700	154,700
Administration	97,400	97,300	97,300	97,400	389,400
	198,500	198,500	198,500	198,500	794,000
Total expenses	$ 564,700	$ 601,000	$ 640,500	$ 769,800	$2,576,000
Pretax profit (loss)	($ 21,300)	($ 37,400)	($ 48,800)	($ 74,300)	($ 33,200)
Provision for federal and state taxes					
Net profit or (loss)	($ 21,300)	($ 37,400)	($ 48,800)	($ 74,300)	($ 33,200)
Cash flow					
Net profit or (loss) from above	($ 21,300)	($ 37,400)	($ 48,800)	($ 74,300)	($ 33,200)
Add:					
Provision for tax					
Depreciation	121,600	144,000	166,500	188,900	621,000
Deferred receipts from installations	25,400	23,200	20,900	18,700	88,200
Cash flow	$ 125,700	$ 129,800	$ 138,600	$ 281,900	$ 676,000

Exhibit 10-3 Projection of Income and Cash Flow

	Third year				
	First Quarter	Second Quarter	Third Quarter	Fourth Quarter	Total Year
Number of subscribers	20,196	22,440	24,684	26,928	26,928
Income					
From subscribers	$ 990,700	$ 945,000	$ 922,300	$1,257,800	$4,115,800
From installations	19,500	21,700	23,900	26,100	91,200
Total income	$1,010,200	$ 966,700	$ 946,200	$1,283,900	$4,207,000
Expenses					
Programming	$ 396,300	$ 378,000	$ 368,900	$ 503,100	$1,646,300
Rental, Telephone company facilities	58,300	65,100	71,800	78,600	273,800
	454,600	443,100	440,700	581,700	1,920,100
Depreciation					
Transmission cable	35,000	39,000	43,100	47,100	164,200
Hookups	70,000	78,100	86,200	94,200	328,500
Hookup units	89,400	99,600	109,800	120,200	419,000
Transmission center equipment	17,000	17,000	17,000	17,000	68,000
	211,400	233,700	256,100	278,500	979,700
General and administrative					
Promotional expenses	62,500	62,500	62,500	62,400	249,900
Engineering	46,800	46,800	46,900	46,900	187,400
Administration	105,700	105,700	105,700	105,700	422,800
	215,000	215,000	215,100	215,000	860,100
Total expenses	$ 881,000	$ 891,800	$ 911,900	$1,075,200	$3,759,900
Pretax profit (loss)	$ 129,200	$ 74,900	$ 34,300	$ 208,700	$ 447,100
Provision for federal and state taxes					
Net profit or (loss)	$ 129,200	$ 74,900	$ 34,300	$ 208,700	$ 447,100
Cash flow					
Net profit or (loss) from above	129,200	74,900	34,300	208,700	447,100
Add:					
Provision for tax Depreciation	211,400	233,700	256,100	278,500	979,700
Deferred receipts from installations	16,400	14,200	12,000	9,800	52,400
Cash flow	$ 357,000	$ 322,800	$ 302,400	$ 497,000	$1,479,200

Exhibit 10-4 Projection of Income and Cash Flow

	Fourth year				
	First Quarter	Second Quarter	Third Quarter	Fourth Quarter	Total Year
Number of subscribers	29,172	31,416	33,660	35,910	35,910
Income					
From subscribers	$1,448,500	$1,331,800	$1,267,900	$1,688,600	$5,736,800
From installations	28,400	30,700	32,900	35,900	127,900
Total income	$1,476,900	$1,362,500	$1,300,800	$1,724,500	$5,864,700
Expenses					
Programming	$ 579,400	$ 532,700	$ 507,200	$ 675,400	$2,294,700
Rental, Telephone company facilities	85,300	92,000	98,700	105,500	381,500
	664,700	624,700	605,900	780,900	2,676,200
Depreciation					
Transmission cable	51,200	55,200	59,200	63,300	228,900
Hookups	102,300	110,400	118,500	126,500	457,700
Hookup units	130,400	140,800	151,100	161,400	583,700
Transmission center equipment	17,000	17,000	17,000	17,000	68,000
	300,900	323,400	345,800	368,200	1,338,300
General and administrative					
Promotional expenses	62,500	62,500	62,400	28,800	216,200
Engineering	52,300	52,300	52,400	52,400	209,400
Administration	114,100	114,100	114,000	114,000	456,200
	228,900	228,900	228,800	195,200	881,800
Total expenses	$1,194,500	$1,177,000	$1,180,500	$1,344,300	$4,896,300
Pretax profit (loss)	$ 282,400	$ 185,500	$ 120,300	$ 380,200	$ 968,400
Provision for federal and state taxes		39,500	72,200	228,100	339,800
Net profit or (loss)	$ 282,400	$ 146,000	$ 48,100	$ 152,100	$ 628,600
Cash flow					
Profit or (loss) from above	$ 282,400	$ 146,000	$ 48,100	$ 152,100	$ 628,600
Add:					
Provision for tax		39,600	72,100	228,100	339,800
Depreciation	300,900	323,400	345,800	368,200	1,338,300
Deferred receipts from installations	7,500	5,200	3,100	100	15,900
Cash flow	$ 590,800	$ 514,200	$ 469,100	$ 748,500	$2,322,600

The revenues from subscribers, although projected on the basis of $180 per year or $15 per month, have been adjusted to reflect seasonal viewing habits. The monthly viewing index has been applied to the three months of each quarter to accomplish this.

Start-up costs are not included in the statements. They are included in Exhibit 10-5, however. The cash flow reflected in Exhibits 10-1 through 10-4 shows the flow from ongoing operations only. (It must be remembered that deferred taxes included as cash flow must be paid at some later date and that equipment must also be replaced periodically.)

Projected Capital Requirements

Exhibit 10-5 summarizes all the capital needs over the four-year period and during the start-up period as well. Although the net capital requirement for the entire period is shown as $7,908,788 in the fourth quarter of the fourth year, the peak amount is $8,116,573 in the third quarter of the fourth year.

Although the data in Exhibits 10-1 through 10-5 are important in evaluation of the profit opportunities in this new venture, a more probing analysis beyond this is needed. The information for such an analysis is provided through determination of the breakeven point, a discussion of which follows.

Determining the Breakeven Point

The first step is to select a time period in which the data and conditions represent normal operations. Because all the four years that have been projected include periods of growth, the figures shown in Exhibits 10-1 through 10-4 were not used. In making the breakeven analysis shown in Table 10-13, it was assumed that all 35,910 subscribers were hooked up and that all installations, except for normal turnover and population growth, were completed.

The second step is the identification of costs that are variable and those that are relatively fixed. This breakdown was made as follows.

Exhibit 10-5   Projected Capital Requirements

	Payments to Telephone Company	Hookups	Hookup Units	Transmission Center	Working Capital	Total Requirements	Cash from Operations	Net capital requirements	
								Period	Cumulative
Start-up period	$ 510,000			680,000	75,000	1,265,000	(304,650)	1,569,650	1,569,650
First year									
First quarter		128,000	412,750			540,750	(105,492)	646,242	2,215,892
Second quarter	510,000	128,000	412,750			1,050,750	(61,061)	1,111,811	3,327,703
Third quarter		128,000	412,750			540,750	(25,380)	566,130	3,899,833
Fourth quarter		128,000	412,750			540,750	66,847	473,903	4,367,736
Total first year	1,020,000	512,000	1,651,000	680,000	75,000	3,938,000	(429,736)	4,367,736	
Second year									
First quarter		128,000	412,750			540,750	125,756	414,994	4,782,730
Second quarter	510,000	128,000	412,750			1,050,750	129,794	920,956	5,703,686
Third quarter		128,000	412,750			540,750	138,547	402,203	6,105,889
Fourth quarter		128,000	412,750			540,750	281,938	258,812	6,364,701
Total second year	510,000	512,000	1,651,000			2,673,000	676,035	1,996,965	
Third year									
First quarter		128,000	412,750			540,750	356,978	183,772	6,548,473
Second quarter	510,000	128,000	412,750			1,050,750	322,814	727,936	7,276,409
Third quarter		128,000	412,750			540,750	302,449	238,301	7,514,710
Fourth quarter		128,000	412,750			540,750	497,003	43,747	7,558,457
Total third year	510,000	512,000	1,651,000			2,673,000	1,479,244	1,193,756	

Exhibit 10-5 (Continued)

	Payments to Telephone Company	Hookups	Hookup Units	Transmission Center	Working Capital	Total Requirements	Cash from Operations	Net capital requirements Period	Net capital requirements Cumulative
Fourth year									
First quarter		128,000	412,750			540,750	590,876	(50,126)	7,508,331
Second quarter	510,000	128,000	412,750			1,050,750	514,132	536,618	8,044,949
Third quarter		128,000	412,750			540,750	469,126	71,624	8,116,573[a]
Fourth quarter		128,000	412,750			540,750	748,535	(207,785)	7,908,788
Total fourth year	510,000	512,000	1,651,000			2,673,000	2,322,669	350,331	
	2,550,000	2,048,000	6,604,000	680,000	75,000	11,957,000	4,048,212	7,908,788	

[a] Peak capital requirements.

Table 10-13   Breakeven Analysis

	Total Based on Completed System	Breakeven	Excess above Breakeven
Number of subscribers	35,910	23,232	12,678
Income from subscribers	$6,463,800	$4,181,738	$2,282,062
Variable expenses			
Programming	2,585,520	1,672,695	912,825
Rental of telephone facilities	430,920	279,006	151,914
Routemen (general and administrative)	130,500	84,387	46,113
Total	3,146,940	2,036,088	1,110,852
Contribution to profit	3,316,860	2,145,650	1,171,210
Fixed expenses			
Promotional	115,200	115,200	
Depreciation	1,495,400	1,495,400	
Engineering	209,350	209,350	
General and administrative	325,700	325,700	
	2,145,650	2,145,650	
Pretax Profit	$1,171,210		$1,171,210

Variable Expenses

Programming costs, rental of telephone facilities, and expenses relating to salaries, payroll-related costs, and automobile expenses of the routemen were considered to be variable with the revenue from subscribers.

Fixed Expenses

Promotional expenses, depreciation, engineering, and general and administrative expenses exclusive of the collection function were considered to be fixed. Promotional expenses included 7 salesmen rather than the 18 that were projected during the period of growth. The related payroll expenses and automobile costs were adjusted accordingly.

Variable expenses amount to 48.7% (rounded) of subscriber income, leaving 51.3% of the income to cover fixed costs and profits. By dividing 51.3% into the fixed expenses of $2,145,650, we obtain a breakeven point of $4,181,738 in revenues (23,232 subscribers).

The pretax profit on all income above the breakeven level is 51.3% of such additional revenues. Conversely, the loss would be 51.3% of every dollar by which revenues fall below breakeven. If any additional sales above breakeven apply to subscribers outside the existing system, then the need for additional fixed costs must be taken into account. This would change the breakeven point and the profit calculations.

With these basic facts available, various assumptions can be made. Should revenues per subscriber be lower than $180 per year, for example, the new breakeven point could be easily recalculated to reveal the effect on profitability. If programming costs should be higher (or lower), this adjustment can also be made.

Summary of Key Financial Data

The key financial information required to evaluate the profit potential of this venture is summarized in Table 10-14.

Table 10-14   Key Financial Data

	Number of Subscribers	Income from Subscribers ($)	Cumulative Capital Requirements ($)	Pretax Profit ($)	Percent Return on		Turnover of Capital (times)
					Income from Subscribers	Capital	
First year	8,976	863	4368	(511)	(59.7)	(11.7)	5.1
Second year	17,952	2487	6365	(33)	(1.3)	(.5)	2.6
Third year	26,928	4116	7558	447	10.7	5.9	1.8
Fourth year	35,910	5737	8117	968	16.8	11.9	1.4
completed system[a]	35,910	6464	8117	1171	18.7	14.4	1.3

[a] Since the full 35,910 subscriber installations were not completed until the end of the fourth year, these figures were included to give effect to a full year's results.

With the availability of this type of information, the management of the proposed venture has the basic financial data required to make a decision as to whether it should embark on the proposed venture in pay TV. There is no pat rule as to the return that should be expected in a business—this is a management decision because only the management knows what its goals are. It must evaluate the market potential, competition, and the problems in the business along with its goals. In the pay TV industry, for example, certain uncertainties exist with respect to the question of paying copyright fees on programs that emanate from other broadcast sources. Also, strong resistance is shown by conventional television and theaters. All these factors must be evaluated and weighed before a decision is made. Then, even if unanticipated problems do arise, the new company will be better prepared to cope with them.

CHAPTER 11

UTILIZATION OF INVESTMENT AND ITS RELATION TO PROFITABILITY

The key to profitability is the effective utilization of investment. Good control of inventories and efficient utilization of facilities contributes far more to profitability than comparing dollars spent with dollars budgeted.

Effective utilization of the investment of a business is probably the most important single factor affecting profitability. The greater the investment, the greater the impact of utilization on the profits of the business.

Modern-day commuter railroads are a good illustration of a high investment business that suffers badly from under utilization. Locomotives of one commuter line in the eastern part of the country are used slightly more than one-third of the time, while passenger cars roll less than 20% of the time. Even train crews are effectively used less than half the hours for which they are paid. As might be expected, this railroad, similar to several other commuter lines, is being heavily subsidized by the government. Sometimes, effective utilization of investment is hampered by conditions outside the control of the business—as in the case of heavy air traffic congestion. One domestic airline estimated that during peak travel months delays add $1 million per month to its costs, including approximately $200,000 each month for extra fuel required while circling the airport area. As in the case of train crews, underutilization of investment is frequently accompanied by other costs not directly related to utilization.

Underutilization and the accompanying loss of profitability can also result from short runs—be they production runs or the average haul distance of an airline. A short haul airline is more than likely far less profitable for an average haul of, say, 450 miles, as compared with the industry average of 700 miles.

The problems of utilization are not limited to high investment businesses such as railroads and airlines. All business enterprises are affected by volume of activity. Our discussion in this chapter is directed to the manufacturing enterprise.

INVESTMENT IS A VARIABLE FACTOR

When business activity moves past 85% of capacity, most managements begin thinking seriously of increasing capacity to accommodate a higher volume of production. During a period of recession, volume can drop to 70% of capacity or lower.

Increases in production volume (or rendering services) can take various forms. If there is a question as to permanency of rising demand, expansion might take the form of overtime work—or an additional shift might be added. This permits expansion without increasing the investment in facilities. Expansion can also be accomplished by purchase of more modern equipment without expanding the physical plant. If additional space is needed, or if the labor market is no longer satisfactory, the company may make a decision to relocate.

The decision as to which of these alternatives is the most desirable must be tempered by consideration of the effect on profits of the various alternatives. If the facilities are expanded, for example, and the anticipated sales volume does not materialize, the cost of the added facilities becomes a deterrent to improved earnings. The decision to expand, then, is a calculated risk at best.

It is possible, however, to make certain evaluations as to the impact of volume (or lack of volume) on profits. The determination of profit-volume relationships under various alternatives can be a helpful aid in reducing the risk factor in making decisions of this nature.

Each sales dollar a customer pays for goods and services includes an allowance for reimbursing the seller for his fixed expenses. The amount of profit accruing to the seller is dependent to a large extent upon the relationship of the allowance for fixed costs provided for in the selling price to the fixed costs actually incurred.

When the marginal income (total sales dollars less variable costs) is equal to fixed costs, we have a breakeven situation. This is illustrated in Exhibit 11-1 at the 70% capacity level.

Exhibit 11-1   Profits at Various Levels of Capacity

	70% Capacity	80% Capacity	85% Capacity	90% Capacity
Sales volume	$700,000	$800,000	$850,000	$900,000
Variable costs	315,000	360,000	382,500	405,000
Marginal income	$385,000	$440,000	$467,500	$495,000
Fixed costs	385,000	385,000	385,000	385,000
Profit		$ 55,000	$ 82,500	$110,000
Percent Profit		6.9	9.7	12.2

At the 80% capacity level, the amount by which the marginal income exceeds the actual fixed costs ($440,000 minus $385,000) equals profit ($55,000 or 6.9% of sales). At the 85 and 90% capacity levels, the amounts for the same items are $82,500 and $110,000, respectively, or 9.7 and 12.2% of sales. This example illustrates the effect of increased utilization of facilities on profits assuming other things are equal.

EFFECT OF INCREASED CAPACITY ON PROFITS

Frequently, when management finds that the company is operating at levels exceeding 90% of capacity, it decides to expand. Once new facilities are added, what previously represented 90% capacity may be, say, 75% of the expanded facilities. Obviously, an expansion of capacity without increasing sales volume reduces profits, as borne out by the figures in Exhibit 11-2.

Exhibit 11-2   Effect of Expanded Capacity on Profits

	70% Capacity	80% Capacity	85% Capacity	90% Capacity
Sales volume	$700,000	$800,000	$850,000	$900,000
Variable costs	315,000	360,000	382,500	405,000
Marginal income	$385,000	$400,000	$467,500	$495,000
Fixed costs	425,000	425,000	425,000	425,000
Profit	($ 40,000)	$ 15,000	$ 42,500	$ 70,000
Percent profit		1.9	5.0	7.8

Note that profits have decreased by the additional amount of fixed costs required to expand productive capacity. A comparison of both exhibits follows.

Sales Volume ($)	Profits before Expansion ($)	Profits after Expansion ($)
700,000		(40,000)
800,000	55,000	15,000
850,000	82,500	42,500
900,000	110,000	70,000

Computations such as these can never answer the question whether to expand facilities or by how much to expand. But they can give a good indication of the effect on profits if the expansion program goes through and additional sales volume does not fulfill expectations.

OVERTIME IN LIEU OF EXPANSION

When there are indications that planned expansion of facilities may not be followed by sufficient increases in volume, many companies resort to the use of overtime. A 10-hour day, for example, results in 25% more working hours.

Often, however, the economics of working overtime is questionable because of the premium pay when employees are paid time-and-a-half. To determine whether overtime is feasible, it is necessary to compare the added premium cost of labor with the amount of fixed costs that will be absorbed in the added production. While the example that follows considers only the premium cost of overtime, there are other possible additional costs, such as fringe benefits or shift differential pay. It has been assumed, however, that fixed costs remain unchanged.

Overtime Pay Computation

Department A has 200 employees working a 40-hour week. At an hourly rate of $2.50, the total straight-time payroll for a 21-day month amounts to $84,000. To obtain an additional 10% production, the increase in the straight-time payroll would be $8400. At time-and-a-half, the premium pay therefore would be $4200.

Fixed Cost Absorption Computation

If production were to be increased in Department A by 10% with no expenditure for additional equipment, existing fixed costs would be absorbed by increased production. If existing fixed costs were $56,000 per month, the amount absorbed by increased production would be 10% of $56,000, or $5600.

Since the overtime over and above straight-time amounts to $4200, while the fixed costs absorbed into the additional production are $5600, there is a gain of $1400 through working overtime.

FALLACY OF EXCESS EQUIPMENT

Over a period of years, companies accumulate machines which have long since been replaced by newer models. The rationale for retaining such equipment is that the extra capacity "comes in handy" during peak periods when customers are demanding shipment of their orders. This argument is often reinforced by computations which show that the hourly cost of operating such equipment is miniscule.

One company divided the depreciation on excess machinery by the number of available machine hours in the year. There were 12 machines whose annual depreciation was $24,000. This was divided by 2000 hours per machine, or a total of 24,000 machine hours per year, to arrive at an hourly cost of $1. At such a low cost, who could argue with the justification of holding on to the equipment?

The true facts of the case were that the 12 machines occupied about 5000 square feet, which forced the company to rent space on the outside for storage of raw materials. The rental of this outside space plus the watchman service, extra insurance, cleaning service, and utilities added approximately $12,000 per year to the overhead cost. In addition, an extra maintenance man was tied up servicing the 12 machines. His wages with fringes amounted to $8000 per year. Thus the annual cost of keeping the 12 machines was not $24,000 but $44,000.

Furthermore, a study of the hours of use indicated that the equipment was operated 3800 hours per year rather than 24,000. Management's evaluation of $1 per machine hour as the operating cost turned out to be closer to $12 per hour ($44,000 ÷ 3,800 hours).

This example should not be construed to mean that excess equipment is never justified. There are many instances when frequent changeovers from one set of tools to another justify extra machines even if utilization is lowered. By leaving tools in the machine until the next run, high costs required in the setup and teardown operations can be eliminated.

While there is a point of diminishing returns in retaining excess equipment, no pat formula can be applied to determine that point. Each instance must be judged on its own merits.

MONITORING THE UTILIZATION OF EQUIPMENT

During the past decade more and more companies have dismantled old plants and moved into new facilities often located in a different part of the country. Such moves are usually accompanied by replacement of existing machines with newer and faster equipment. Machine utilization is frequently lowered when moves are made. The following are some of the reasons for the decrease in utilization.

- The labor force in the new location may be entirely unfamiliar with machine operation, particularly when one operator is expected to tend several machines and to monitor the quality of the product being fabricated.
- Setup and maintenance men are usually not available in sufficient numbers. Those who are available may have to be trained. The inability of the company to fill the need for such men is reflected in the efficiency with which the machines can be operated.
- The introduction of tools and equipment of greater precision makes the problems of the setup man and the toolmaker even more critical and makes necessary a larger quality assurance staff.

Pinpointing poor machine utilization raises questions that can lead to quicker solutions of chronic problems than might otherwise be obtained. Some examples are:

- Utilization reports revealed that an operator charged with tending six machines could not maintain the desired rate of utilization because the machines were spread over a 50-foot area. Naturally, utilization dropped with no corresponding reduction in direct labor cost.
- Watching utilization reports pointed up to to one plant manager that the cataloging and storage of tools were so inefficient that delays frequently occurred while tools were being sought. As a remedial measure, the floor area of the tool crib was tripled and an additional man assigned to assure that tools could be found when needed. The returned tools were inspected to assure that they would be in good condition when reissued.
- In another situation monitoring the utilization of equipment on a systematic and analytical basis revealed that machines in one department could not function at full capacity because of shortages in material flowing to it from another department. When the situation occurred frequently, management had to decide whether to add another machine in the deficient department, increase the hours of operation of the existing equipment, or subcontract some of the work.

Many companies, particularly those using expensive automated equipment, have found that the machine utilization report is one of the most important management control tools of all the reports available to them. Such a report is discussed in the section that follows.

PREPARATION OF UTILIZATION REPORT

The purpose of a utilization report, stated simply, is to compare the actual hours that a machine or group of similar machines operates with the number of hours that it should operate. The determination of the number of hours machines should have been run is dependent on what should reasonably be expected. For instance, when equipment is purchased, certain minimum standards of output are established to justify the purchase. A very expensive machine, for example, may be required to operate two or three shifts in order to justify its purchase. Using this type of data as a guideline, with a further adjustment to allow for a reasonable amount of downtime for changeovers, adjustments, and repairs, the utilization hours can be determined. Exhibit 11–3 shows how the utilization base can be determined. The daily or weekly comparison of this figure with actual hours provides management with a useful control tool.

Note in the exhibit that the types of machines are listed with the number of shifts indicated. These are the shifts assumed when the equipment was purchased. Should management now find that it cannot justify operating this number of shifts, it will find itself at a competitive disadvantage.

The number of machines multiplied by the number of daily hours of operation yields the machine hours available per day. Obviously, no company can operate all its machines for all the hours that such a calculation shows. An adjustment is needed to reduce the available hours to a more realistic figure which takes into account the changeover time, time needed for repairs to equipment and other normal delays that cannot be avoided. Ideally, the determination of the amount of adjustment should be based on records of machine downtime by cause. If such records are not available, an estimate should be made by an industrial engineer or foreman familiar with the equipment. This adjustment can best be expressed as a percentage.

Exhibit 11-3 Calculation of Machine Hours

Equipment	Machines Available for Production	Number of Shifts	Machine Hours Available per Day	Utilization of Equipment (%)	Machine Hours per Day Available for Production
Compression molding					
Rotaries	16	3	384	75	288
Stokes	9	3	216	81	176
Transfer press	8	3	192	63	121
Strauss	10	3	240	75	180
Total	43	3	1032	74	765
Injection molding					
4-Ounce	6	3	144	80	115
8 and 12-Ounce	3	3	72	70	50
96-Ounce	1	3	24	60	14
Total	10	3	240	74	179
Assembly					
Automatic stakers	9	2	144	70	101
Semiautomatic and hand stakers	4	2	64	70	45
Semiautomatic and hand stakers	4	1	32	70	22
Closure liners	6	1	48	75	36
Total	23	—	288	71	204
Metal fabrication					
Z & H, 9-ton presses	18	1	144	28	40
V & O, #0, #1, 25-ton, and 50-ton	8	1	64	28	18
Minister, 22-ton	5	1	40	28	11
Benchmaster, 4-ton and B & J	3	1	24	28	8
Brandeis, 30-ton	1	1	8	28	2
Henry & Wright, 60-ton	1	1	8	28	2
Pin machines	9	2	144	90	124
Total	45	—	432	47	205

The available hours for production are determined by multiplying available hours by the percentage of utilization.

The metal fabrication section in Exhibit 11–3 shows only a 28% utilization factor, which raises questions as to credibility. This is an illustration of a situation where excess equipment is maintained to reduce setup and changeover requirements. Since the management is satsfied that the low utilization is offset by other savings, the resulting machine hours based on 28% utilization can be used as a norm for this group.

With the basic machine hours determined for the various types of equipment illustrated in Exhibit 11–3, the only step left is to accumulate the actual hours of operation of the various types of equipment and to compare these with the norm. This can be done on a daily basis for problem areas until the situation is remedied, and on a weekly basis for other areas.

INTERPLAY OF UTILIZATION AND EFFICIENCY

Once machine utilization has been brought within a reasonable degree of control and major periods of downtime have been eliminated, management should focus more of its attention on machine productivity during the hours the machines are running. It is entirely possible that a machine being reported as operating at 100% utilization could in actuality be producing at a substantially lower percentage of efficiency because:

- Periods reported as running hours may not be producing product because the material may be feeding improperly.
- Machines with variable speed controls may be running at lower speeds.
- Short periods of downtime may be reported as running time, resulting in overstatement of the hours reported as running time. This may be desirable in order to eliminate paperwork.

Exhibit 11–4 illustrates alternative methods of reporting, which can show utilization and machine efficiency at variance with each other.

Exhibit 11-4   Comparison of Alternative Methods of Reporting[a]

Reporting Procedure A		Reporting Procedure B	
Running hours	70	Running hours	49
Machine utilization		Machine utilization	
(70 ÷ 70)	100%	(49 ÷ 70)	70%
Standard production		Standard production	
70 hours × 300		49 hours × 300	
per hour	21,000	per hour	14,700
Actual units produced	14,700	Actual units produced	14,700
Machine efficiency		Machine efficiency	
14,700/21,000	70%	14,700/14,700	100%
Overall Efficiency		Overall efficiency	
Machine utilization ×		Machine utilization ×	
machine efficiency	70%	machine efficiency	70%

[a] Assumptions: total available hours, 70; standard production per hour, 300.

Although in the first instance, reporting procedure A, the utilization is shown as 100% because the machine has been reported as running 70 hours against an available number of 70 hours, the comparison of actual units produced with the number that should have been produced if the machine had run 70 hours reveals that the machine, while running, operated at an efficiency of 70%. The overall percentage, obtained by multiplying the utilization percentage by the efficiency percentage, comes to 70% (100% times 70%).

Under reporting procedure B, in which running hours are accounted for on a more meticulous basis, the utilization percentage is shown as 70%. The standard units of production therefore are based on 49 running hours rather than 70. Therefore, the actual units produced (14,700) compare exactly with the standard based on 49 hours times 300 units per hour. The high machine efficiency precentage offsets the low utilization percentage.

Exhibit 11–4 illustrates that inequities in reporting—a situation that can never be entirely eliminated—require further evaluations of performance which will account for differences in reporting. The equating factor in this instance is the calculation of an overall efficiency percentage.

PRODUCTIVE CAPACITY MORE THAN JUST EQUIPMENT UTILIZATION

In the foregoing discussion, our frame of reference was concentrated on individual units of production equipment. In the evaluation of the overall return on investment, it is necessary to consider units of equipment as a whole rather than on a piecemeal basis. The measure of utilization of equipment then comes closer to a measure of total productive capacity. Other types of investment—inventory, for example,—must also be considered in the measurement of productive capacity.

Businessmen who overexpand, in an effort to tap a rapidly rising demand, find at a certain point that increased competition can result in a sudden drying up of their sales volume. As a result, they are faced with an overcapacity situation. Even when the logical alternative is to cut back, there is frequently great reluctance to do so—for two basic reasons:

1. Expectation that the demand curve will resume its upward climb.
2. Because cutting back capacity would be interpreted as an admission that an error had been made.

OVEREXPANSION—A CASE STUDY

Apex, Inc. (a fictitious name), manufactures office copying equipment and is illustrative of a company that was enjoying a rapid demand for its products. Seeing no immediate limitation to demand, the company built a second plant and purchased another company to broaden its line.

After several years of rapid expansion of facilities and sales—sales increased 10 times (from $3,000,000 annually to $30,000,000), while cost of facilities and inventories increased $11\frac{1}{2}$ times over the same period. Sales, instead of continuing the upward climb suddenly turned downward, to less than $14,000,000, and profits quickly reverted to losses. The reason for this was the success of a large com-

Exhibit 11-5

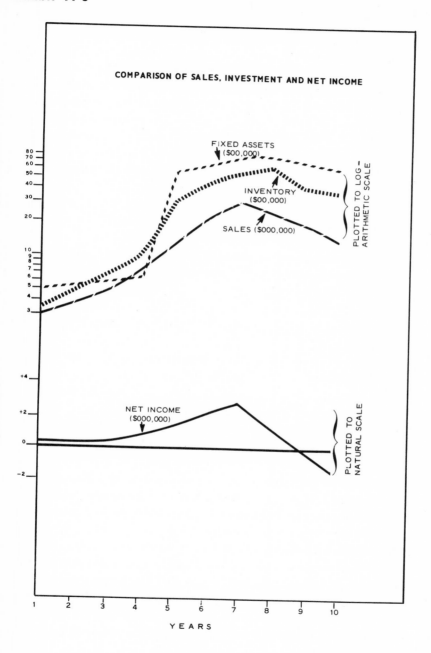

petitor in developing a copier that used ordinary unsensitized paper. This cut sharply into the sales of all manufacturers of conventional copying machines.

Apex, in a belated review of the basic factors, realized how badly inventories and fixed assets had outstripped the growth of sales. Exhibit 11–5 shows sales, inventories, and fixed assets plotted on a logarithmic scale—emphasizing percentage rather than absolute dollar relationships, and thus facilitating comparison of the rate of growth.

The chart shows dramatically how the increase in inventories and fixed assets outstripped the growth of sales. As soon as sales turned down in the seventh year, profits quickly reverted to losses.

The Retrenchment Program

The company acknowledged that it had overextended itself through too rapid expansion of facilities and turned its attention to a program of retrenchment. The marketing department had been asked for a realistic appraisal of the company's share of the market. After considering the various competitive factors, an estimate was made that sales would stabilize at $10 to $12 million per year.

Since the sales volume was about evenly split between the eastern and midwestern plant—and since both were about the same size— the decision was made to move all facilities to the midwestern location. Either plant could provide room for further expansion to about $15,000,000 per year. In the event that further expansion beyond this level was required, both plants had ample area for additional construction.

The decision to consolidate at the midwestern facilities was based on the observation that this had always been the more profitable of the two locations. The company felt it would gain because the less profitable of the two plants would then be disposed of—further narrowing down the losses.

Selection of the midwestern location proved to be erroneous. What the company had failed to recognize was that the greater profitability of the midwestern plant was due to its being favored with the longer runs. The eastern plant had the bulk of the technical knowhow and it ran the less profitable, more difficult, short runs—which were eventually transferred to the other plant when demand increased and the "bugs" were worked out. Most of the employees with the know-how would not move out of the East—this meant that the company lost many of its experienced employees with the resulting detrimental effect on the profitability of the products produced in the East.

The move to the Midwest was carried out—with the result that quality on many of the more difficult products deteriorated badly and customer rejections increased. Development of new products almost ceased. Sales, instead of stabilizing at $10 to $12 million, dropped to $7 million.

The new management of the company recognized that it could not reverse the decision made by its predecessors. It therefore embarked on an extensive training program to recover the knowhow it had lost.

The entry of the new copier and its effect on the existing types being manufactured could not have accurately been predicted. Apex, along with many of its competitors, could not have avoided a serious deterioration in its sales volume. However, had Apex confined its expansion within the existing facilities in the East, it would not have found retrenchment so painful. Additionally, and even more important, it would not have lost the technical personnel so necessary in this age of research.

PLAN, PROGRAM, POLICE

Profits are very closely related to the effectiveness with which a company utilizes its facilities. Although this chapter prescribes methods that can be used in measuring the effect on profits of changes in capacity, pure arithmetic is not the only criterion for making management decisions. Increases in facilities may mean introduction of labor-saving equipment which would change the variable cost content in the product. Thus an increase in capacity without a commensurate increase in sales volume may not always result in fewer profits.

Another consideration is the greater flexibility of the existing labor force when modern equipment which produces a more uniform product is added. Such equipment reduces the number of new employees required, which in turn reduces the training costs and loss of production incurred with new untrained employees. Spoilage becomes a smaller factor in cost not only because of a larger cadre of skilled employees but because the equipment is more efficient. Quality assurance costs, a major item in a manufacturing operation, are also reduced because of the greater uniformity of the product.

In its efforts to maximize profits in a dog-eat-dog economy, management cannot limit its investigations merely to cost savings through conventional cost reduction procedures. It must also focus on growth. The rate of growth must be as fast or faster than that of the industry, but it cannot become an end in itself. Growth must be planned, programmed, and policed.

CHAPTER 12

THE ECONOMY AND ITS EFFECT ON PROFITABILITY

The impact that the state of the economy can have on profits is well known. Herein lies the clue as to whether modern business should make its plans based on one set of assumptions or whether plans should be formulated through a recognition of the range of possibilities based on both an optimistic and a pessimistic look at the future.

The modern-day professional manager is continually under pressure to make his business more competitive. If industry in general is increasing capacity, he too is compelled to increase the productive capacity of his company to retain its share of the market. This may call for plant relocation with its attendant problems of training new employees, purchasing new equipment, investing in research and development, and borrowing additional funds. All these fall into the category of planning, which can have long term effects. It is the magnitude of the long term effects that bears closely upon whether an individual company will survive or fall by the wayside during a period of economic retrenchment.

An executive dares not take too conservative a stance for fear that inaction will cause substantial loss of profits. This was illustrated during the 1950s when Sewell Avery, head of Montgomery Ward, held up expansion because he anticipated a depression. His plan was to wait until costs dropped and a more favorable climate for expansion developed.

Mr. Avery's thesis was predicated on the assumption that the same economic trends that followed World War I would repeat themselves after World War II. His expectations might have been realized had not the cold war period and the impact of spending for the space effort heated up the postwar boom to even higher peaks of economic activity—factors that were difficult to assess except in retrospect.

However, Sewell Avery's experience should not be used as an excuse for throwing caution to the winds and moving blindly ahead without considering alternatives, particularly since strains in our economy have been obvious—as has been apparent in our monetary system.

Executives who keep their "ear to the ground" and sense impending changes take a middle course when clouds appear on the horizon. This permits them to consider alternatives. Corporate profits are highly sensitive to national economic activity. During expansionary periods they increase at a faster rate than national income. During periods when the national income drops, profits can quickly revert to losses.

The National Industrial Conference Board's "Profits in Perspective," which was prepared for the 37th Annual Meeting of the Conference Board, points out that even in good times there is no assurance of reward for risk. During the peak of prosperity in 1929, for example, about 41% of all active corporations wound up their operations with a deficit. At the depths of the depression, four out of every five corporations could not report net income. In fact, 10 years after the start of the depression, the number of corporations reporting losses was substantially greater than those reporting taxable income.

The memorable decade of low economic activity came to an end with the outbreak of World War II. The pent-up demand for products that were in short supply during the war, the firing up of the economy by both the Korean and Vietnam wars, and the massive expenditures for the space program, raised the economic activity to fever pitch during the 1950s and 1960s. The 1960s, particularly, were just as extreme in one direction as the 1930s were in the other. This long period of prosperity has resulted in a generation of managers nurtured in an ever-growing and ever-expanding economy. This type of expansion tends to mask inefficiencies and waste. In such an economy today's excess inventories might well become tomorrow's backlog. Today's surplus personnel can become tomorrow's recruitment prospects if we merely bide our time. This is not true of an economy that is phasing downward into a recession.

Business cycles are an inherent part of our capitalistic system, a fact of life that is too easily overlooked. Since our business community has experienced an unusually prolonged period of expansion in the 1960s, it is too easy to become entranced with the momentum of forward movement only. It would be fitting, therefore, to prepare for the unexpected.

The Business Cycle

No reference to recessionary trends is complete without a brief review of the business cycle, recession being only one phase of that cycle. A good point of reference might be the recovery from a preceding recession, which in its later stages becomes the beginning of the next rise. As the recovery stage ends and the rise gains momentum, business begins to approach capacity. Profits increase because additional sales volume is obtained with a minimum of additional cost. As profits become larger, more competitors enter the field and competition becomes keener. Existing facilities become strained in the attempt of each producer to obtain a larger share of the market. As a result, additional facilities are built, and new, more modern equipment is installed. With the increased expansion, the boom swings into high gear; labor becomes more scarce; wages rise higher and higher, driving prices upward. Along with increased sales go increased inventories which also are accumulated at increasingly higher costs.

At a certain point in every boom, governmental controls notwithstanding, demand begins to slow down. This point is reached as soon as the consumer has purchased too many of the goods that he normally would not have bought until a year or two later. Demand falls off while the consumer "catches up." If the catching-up period is prolonged, possibly because of increased pessimism and loss of confidence in the future, inventories and fixed costs suddenly loom large because the sales they were intended to support have evaporated.

Prices are reduced to dispose of excess inventories. As prices are reduced, marginal producers are forced out of business; their inventories and facilities becoming a glut on the market, driving prices still lower. As business cuts back and unemployment increases, consumers who have overextended themselves begin to liquidate. In short, they sell houses that are now too expensive to carry; they return automobiles and appliances on which they can no longer make installment payments; and they begin to hoard money instead of spending it. All this results in a further depressing effect on the economy as liquidation accelerates and the forces of recession reign supreme.

IMPACT OF THE ECONOMY ON PROFITS

The impact that various phases of the economy can have on profits is well known. Herein lies the clue as to whether a modern business should make its plans based on one set of assumptions, or whether plans should be formulated through a recognition of the range of possibilities based on both an optimistic and a pessimistic look at the coming years.

The ability of a management to make a quick turnaround is indicative of a flexible management. Being fully aware of the parameters within which such flexibility should be exercised can be an important ingredient to a more successful business.

SECTION III

Importance of Meaningful Feedback

PRESSURES ON THE PROFESSIONAL MANAGER FOR PROFITS

The professional manager of a publicly owned company is subjected not only to the normal competitive pressures of the marketplace— he is also pressured by the stockholder who demands an optimum return on his investment even though he may have unwisely purchased his stock at too high a price. This chapter reviews some of the steps that can be taken to improve return on investment.

Konrad Lorenz, the Austrian physiologist, in his book, *On aggression*, points out that the modern way of life is a kind of grotesque overdevelopment which violates Nature's laws by continuing growth patterns even though such growth can harm man. The hectic pace of modern men is really not necessary, for they could take things more easily—so goes the theory. Actually, though, slowing down the pace is virtually impossible. Konrad Lorenz further observes that economic and technical overdevelopment in our modern-day society causes many to be subject to the so-called "managerial diseases"— heart attacks, high blood pressure, ulcers, and neuroses.*

The professional manager of a publicly owned company is particularly vulnerable to such pressures—not just because of the normal competitive forces, which in themselves are difficult, but because of pressures exerted by the stockholders for profits. This pressure becomes particularly strong at stockholder meetings when the results for the preceding year are reviewed.

* David C. Anderson, "Policy Riddle: Ecology vs. the Economy," *The Wall Street Journal*, February 2, 1970.

Another facet that makes up the profile of the stockholder is represented by the group whose interest in the company is limited to the desire to obtain an optimum return on stocks owned. It matters little to this investor that he may have unwisely purchased his stock at unprecedented peak prices due to a temporary market advantage which the industry or company enjoyed. He still demands that the company meet dividend payments that furnish an optimum return on his investment on overpriced stock.

Since the number of stockholders is usually large, there is always a pool of available critics who voice dissent at stockholder meetings and apply unreasonable pressures on managements already preoccupied with problems created by the forces of competition (not to be confused with those who play a useful devil's advocate role). This stockholder unwittingly plays the role of distractor—thus playing into the hands of competitors by diverting the attention of management from matters requiring its undivided attention. As profits deteriorate, pressures on management increase.

THE POORER THE PROFITS THE GREATER THE PRESSURES

Each segment of management quickly becomes conscious of the importance of showing a good profit—not only for annual report purposes, but for interim statements which become the measure of progress during the year.

Marketing managers strive to book a large order just before the figures are issued to reflect their efforts at making a contribution. Sometimes the large order is, in desperation, taken on a marginal basis—it increases the sales volume but does little for profits. As a consequence, competitors quickly respond with their own price reductions, so that subsequent orders must likewise be taken at depressed prices; fueling a cycle of price reductions which generate a downward trend of profits in the entire industry.

BORROWING FROM THE FUTURE

A fairly common practice is to work feverishly at the end of month to expedite the shipment of everything possible—even to the point of borrowing from next month's sales in order to meet the budget commitment.

A new management, crusading to clean up the "mess" left by the previous management purposely overdoes the job of writing off costs in order to provide itself a "cushion" which can be drawn on to make the coming year look good. Actually, this can be a misleading ploy.

HOW PROFITS CAN BE IMPROVED

Managers will probably always be plagued by such pressures as:

* Stockholder demands.
* Competitive price erosion.
* Difficulty in obtaining firm sales forecasts to facilitate proper planning of production.
* Frequent interruptions of production schedules to accommodate changes requested by customers.
* Restrictions by the financial officer of the company which prohibit building of inventories during lull periods in order to reduce the peaks.

The nightmares that a professional manager experiences usually find their root in declining profits. Often the condition that caused the declining profits is entirely beyond the control of the manager; it may be a situation being experienced by the entire industry—overcapacity, for example. While there is little that can be done in such circumstances, there are certain positive steps that can be taken in many instances. The professional manager should focus his attention on:

* Proper product pricing practices
* Equipment utilization
* Control of inventories
* Knowledge of costs
* More realistic planning

Because of their importance, each step is explored in greater depth.

PROPER PRODUCT PRICING

There is too great a tendency to substitute gimmickry for common sense—particularly in an important function such as pricing products. The marginal contribution concept, which determines how much of the sales dollar is left to cover fixed costs and profits, after accounting for the direct costs of a product, is a very useful analytical tool. But it can be badly abused when used for pricing.

The danger in using the marginal contribution approach in pricing products is that recovery of fixed costs in the selling price is arbitrarily determined—without regard to the actual investment in facilities required to make the product. The risk lies in the frequent assumption that these costs are there anyway so why bother to associate them with a specific product.

It would be far more logical to determine fixed cost recovery using the same assumption used in justifying purchase of the facilities in the first place. If a purchase of equipment was based on the use of a machine for two full shifts at 80% utilization, for example, then this is the basis that should be used in establishing the cost of the product.

In determining the material cost, the price used for purchased material should be based on economical quantity purchases. Spoilage, likewise, cannot be excessive. Labor, similar to material, must be reasonably efficient.

Market prices do not include a subsidy for inefficiency. Therefore, costs must be based on efficient operations. These costs should then be used as standards to measure performance. Variations from "standard" provide a guide as to how far actual costs are deviating from those costs used in setting the selling price.

IMPROVED EQUIPMENT UTILIZATION

The previous section referred to justification of the purchase of equipment if it could be used for two full shifts at 80% utilization. It follows, then, that there must be some monitoring of the actual number of hours the equipment is productive. In many highly automated operations, if equipment utilization is high, labor and material usage efficiency falls in line. In such instances it may not be necessary to maintain detailed records on labor and material.

There are four basic guidelines that should be followed in maintaining utilization of equipment and facilities at an optimum level. They are:

1. *Keep tooling in good condition.* Upon completion of each job, make certain that tools are inspected prior to placing in the tool crib. Any tool that requires sharpening should be sharpened before being placed in the crib in order to be certain that production won't be held up when the tool is required again. Don't try to squeeze through with an unsharpened tool to save time. You'll only have to rework the parts.

2. *Reduce delays in making first piece checks.* Have some backup people available to make first piece checks when several machines are idle awaiting the results of the test. These can be employees drawn from other assignments at peak periods. Unless you do this, you are liable to have several expensive machines lying idle for hours.

3. *Monitor the quality of production closely.* Reduction of spoilage automatically increases equipment utilization. It reduces waste motion and thereby lowers costs. Spoilage reports should not be mere statistics accumulated for the purpose of making analyses at some later date. Properly prepared spoilage reports give a clue to the reasons for spoilage. Also, watch the returns from customers as a clue to inherent defects in the product.

4. *Keep material flowing.* Avoid bottlenecks in the flow of material through the processes—this always means downtime. Also, keep an eye on the backlog of material at incoming inspection. If there is a delay in processing these items, it could mean subsequent delays all through the plant.

KEEP INVENTORIES UNDER CONTROL

Inventory represents a sizable investment in most companies. Return on investment can be improved by exercising proper controls over inventories. Here are two guides:

1. *Make production changes wisely.* The general manager of one

company had a habit of cutting off production of an item abruptly without letting the various parts on the floor be assembled into a finished product. As a result, a great many subassemblies and components had to be returned to stock—some never to be used again, some so fragile that they were certain to be damaged. The best rule to follow is to run everything through to completion. If this isn't feasible because the end product has become obsolete, then give serious consideration to scrapping all items not usable in the near future.

2. *Integrate the accounting system with production control.* Frequently, accountants develop their own independent set of inventory records and reporting procedures. This results in a duplication of record keeping, which can be expensive and confusing.

Since the production control department is responsible for seeing to it that products are properly scheduled through the factory, their records should be used as the basis for accounting. Actually, the accounting department should place dollar values on production control records.

KNOW YOUR COSTS

It frequently happens that a company or division of a company operates for the first 11 months of the year at a profit only to find at physical inventory time that profits were only phantom profits because the inventory was not being properly relieved. This happens when input into inventory is based on actual costs incurred, but relief is something less than input because of unreported spoilage. During the months in which this underrelief of inventory was taking place, profits were being overstated. At physical inventory time, the required adjustment to the inventory meant that the overstatement of profits had to be adjusted—a circumstance that can be a nightmare to any production manager.

The recommended approach to correcting a situation such as this is to establish standards for the various items made. The input into inventory should be based on the net good production multiplied by standard values. Basing input on net good rather than gross production minimizes the possibility of a phantom profit which must later be corrected. The use of the same standard value for relief of inventory assures that input and output values match.

MORE REALISTIC PLANNING

Forward planning sometimes implies that the past is dead so why look back. Actually, it is characteristic of companies and managements to make the same mistake over and over again. A searching look at the past can frequently be quite revealing. Future planning can be directed to avoid repetition of certain experiences which have proved to be expensive in the past.

SUMMING UP

No human being can do his best work while under great strain; these strains, unfortunately, accelerate in direct proportion to the deceleration of profits. The manager of a business is therefore hard put to reverse the trend of profits. While there are admittedly some situations that he can do nothing about, there are some positive steps that can be taken. These are:

- Improve the utilization of equipment, thereby improving return on investment.
- Keep inventories under control. This reduces the investment and results in an increase in the return on investment, the favorite measure used by the stockholder.
- Make sure your cost system gives you correct costs, thus avoiding phantom profits.
- Profit by mistakes of the past. When you plan ahead, make sure you take a backward look.
- Don't resort to gimmicks in pricing your products. Base your costs on normal volume levels and efficient operations. If you do this, your prices should be competitive and you will be able to use these costs to measure performance.

CHAPTER 14

GETTING BEHIND THE OPERATING STATEMENT

It is not enough to look at the overall figures on profitability. The perceptive manager who is not financially oriented needs a better insight into cost flow, as well as a knowledge of the profitability of his products by class of sale.

The operating statement, also known as the "profit and loss statement" and the "income statement," provides a picture of overall profitability of a business. Similar to our view of the moon with the naked eye, the statement gives us a general idea, such as: The moon is round—it appears to be a perfect circle. But when astronomers focus their telescopes, they see mountains and craters. The astronauts go a step further in providing far more detailed analyses of the composition of the moon and possibly an explanation of the origin of the universe.

The operating statement is, in a sense, similar to our view of the moon with the naked eye. We must go further through special analyses to see the more important details behind the overall profit. These analyses include a better insight into the cost flow as well as a determination of the profitability of the various classes of sales that make up total sales. Accordingly, this chapter is broken down into two sections:

- Cost accounting and cost flow.
- Profitability by class of sale.

To illustrate in greater depth the foregoing factors, we use the simplified operating statement in Table 14-1 as a model.

Table 14-1   Operating Statement

Sales	$1000
Cost of sales	635
Gross profit	365
Selling	75
General and administrative	125
Pretax profit	$ 165

As is typical in many manufacturing companies, cost of sales is the major cost element appearing on the operating statement. We therefore cover this topic first in a discussion of cost accounting and cost flow.

COST ACCOUNTING AND COST FLOW

Cost accounting has been defined as the science of recording business transactions relating to the production of goods and services and formulating these transactions into reports which become a method of measurement and a means of control.

The portion of the operating statement that reflects gross profit is the end product of a series of intermediate accounting transactions which we refer to as "cost flow."

Cost Flow under an Actual Cost System

Cost flow, for purposes of this discussion, starts with manufacturing cost of production and ends with cost of sales. The former represents the material, direct labor and factory overhead costs incurred or put into process during the period, while the latter represents the inventory value of the product that has been sold. The following diagrammatic presentation in "tee" account form demonstrates cost flow in an "actual cost" system.

	Work in process		Finished goods	Cost of sales		Sales
Balance	280	790 → Balance	150	635 → 635		1000
Material	310		→ 790			
Labor	200					
Overhead	375					

The sales of $1000 required a cost of sales in the amount of $635, as shown in Table 14-1. The $635 is also shown as a relief to the finished goods inventory account. The manufacturing cost for the period is $885 represented by the material, direct labor, and factory overhead put into process. Since manufacturing cost is greater than cost of sales by $250, there was a build-up in inventory of an equivalent amount. This is shown in Table 14-2.

Table 14-2   Calculation of Inventory Change

	Work in Process ($)	Finished Goods ($)	Total ($)
Beginning balance	280	150	430
Transfers in	885	790	1675
Total available	1165	940	2105
Transfers out	790	635	1425
Ending balance	375	305	680
Increase or decrease	95	155	250

The beginning inventory of both work in process and finished goods add up to $430. The amounts transferred in ($1675) add up to $2105, representing the amount of available inventory either for further processing or for transfer to cost of sales. Subtracting transfers out from the total available amount, we arrive at the ending inventory of $680.

Since the ending inventory has increased from $430 to $680, this results in a build-up of $250.

The foregoing illustration assumed an actual cost system. Actual costing requires a fair amount of work because it is necessary to determine for each period the actual unit cost of production as a basis for valuing inventories. This represents a good deal of work when a company has numerous products in its line. It is preferable to use predetermined costs or standards and to isolate variations from the standard.

Under a standard cost system, materials are priced at a standard price and the amount of variance determined either at point of purchase (most common) or at point of usage. The amount of material that should be used is determined from the bill of materials. Usually some reasonable allowance is made for spoiled work.

Direct labor requirements for each product are based on the measurement of required hours or minutes through time studies or predetermined tables from which values are selected by the type of motion required. The time requirement is then multiplied by the standard hourly rate for the particular operation.

Indirect materials, indirect labor, and other expenses such as utilities and occupancy cost are related to a denominator such as labor or machine hours. An overhead rate per hour or percentage of standard direct labor is applied to the production to account for this element of cost.

Under a standard cost system, all production and inventories are valued at standard cost. Instead of charging the actual cost of materials issued or labor costs incurred to work in process, the standard cost system charges to work in process the production multiplied by the standard value of such production. The amount of the standard cost put into work in process is compared with the actual cost (usually by element of cost) and a variance is calculated. This variance is usually reflected in the internal statements and is used as a control.

The standard cost system has two major advantages:

- Since production and inventories are valued at standard, valuation is greatly simplified when predetermined costs are used.
- Variances provide a guide to deviations from standards.

A simplified operating statement under a standard cost system is compared in Table 14-3 with the previous one based on an actual cost system.

Table 14-3   Comparison of Operating Statement Format for Actual and Standard Costing

	Actual ($)	Standard ($)
Sales	1000	1000
Cost of sales at standard		590
Variance from standard		45
Total cost of sales (actual)	635	635
Gross profit	365	365

There are several variations of the standard cost format that can be used. The gross profit could be calculated at standard and then reduced by the amount of variance. To provide more detail the variance could be broken down to identify the elements of cost causing the variance, that is, material, direct labor, and overhead.

Cost Flow under a Standard Cost System

The cost flow through the "tee" account demonstrated previously for an actual cost system is shown here for a standard cost system.

```
        Work              Finished          Cost
     in process            goods          of sales         Sales
Balance    280 │ 735  Balance  150 │ 590    590 │          │ 1000
Material   305 │               735 │         45 │          │
Labor      175 │                            ↖            │
Overhead   360 │                                          │
                                           Variance
                            Material     5 │ 45↙
                            Labor       25 │
                            Overhead    15 │
```

The flow of costs through work-in-process and finished goods inventories are the same as previously except that standard, rather than actual, costs are used. The difference between actual and standard costs put into process is charged to the variance account. The variance

Table 14-4 Variance Summary

	Actual ($)	Standard ($)	Variance ($)
Material	310	305	5
Direct labor	200	175	25
Overhead	375	360	15
Total	885	840	45

account is then closed out into the cost of sales account. The calculation of the variances is shown in Table 14-4.

Job Order Cost System

A job order cost system is used when products are made (or projects built) according to specifications established by the customer, as opposed to those products usually made for stock. A finished goods inventory account is therefore not used; completed jobs, or segments thereof, move from work-in-process inventory directly to cost of sales.

Under a job order cost system, costs are identified by the job for which they are incurred. This facilitates the determination of profitability by job as well as identification of the investment in inventory in the same manner. In some instances it may be desirable to break down a job into phases or major segments to permit the monitoring of costs in greater detail, rather than await the completion of the job before profitability is determined.

To provide a comparison of the cost flow under a job system, the cost flow originally shown for the actual cost system is converted to a job cost system under which there are four jobs in progress (or four phases of one job).

As shown in the accompanying illustration, costs put into process are broken down into four jobs, with the total of the four reconcilable to the work-in-process account carried on the balance sheet of the company. In order to obtain the profitability of the individual jobs, both cost of sales and sales are likewise broken down into jobs.

It is possible to use standard costs with a job order cost system, although actual costs are more common. Two approaches can be followed in utilizing standards in a job order cost system:

	Work-in-process control		Cost of sales		Sales	
Balance	280	790	790			1,000
Material	310					
Labor	200					
Overhead	375					

Job #1

Balance	60	125	125			195
Material	75					
Labor	20					
Overhead	40					

Job #2

Balance	75	170	170			285
Material	80					
Labor	30					
Overhead	65					

Job #3

Balance	55	240	240			245
Material	60					
Labor	65					
Overhead	130					

Job #4

Balance	90	255	255			275
Material	95					
Labor	85					
Overhead	140					

- Upon completion of a job, the amount at which the job was bid can be used as the value to transfer the finished product to cost of sales. The balance remaining represents the variance for the job.
- When the units of input can be identified by groups of operations, components, subassemblies, or a phase of the work, standard costs can be assigned as in the previous example of standard costing. A variance between the standard cost at input and the actual cost can be determined.

To make use of standards in a job shop, it is preferable to prepare the bid estimate in sufficient detail to provide "estimates" which can be used as standards—rather than make the preparation of standards a separate task. Frequently, the manufacturing cycle is relatively short and does not permit time to prepare standards.

The variance account can be used in the same manner as previously demonstrated for standard costing. However, under the job order cost system, the identification of variances can be made for each job, as well as by elements of cost within each job.

The actual cost system, the standard cost system, and job order costing, demonstrated with "tee" accounts, fall in the category of absorption costing, which means that fixed or nonvariable costs are included in inventory values. The next section discusses direct costing, a system in which inventories are valued at variable or direct costs with fixed costs being charged directly to cost of sales.

Direct Costing

In Table 14-3 the statement format of an actual and a standard cost system were shown side by side. It might be well to show a direct costing statement format in a similar manner, as is done in Table 14-5. As can be gleaned from Table 14-5, variable or direct costs are deducted from sales to arrive at the contribution to fixed costs and profit. Direct costs include such items as material, direct labor, supplies, and other indirect labor and indirect materials which vary with the level of production.

Table 14-5   Comparison of Operating Statement Format for Direct Costing—"Actual" Versus "Standard"

	Direct Costing Actual ($)	Direct Costing Standard ($)
Sales	1000	1000
Direct costs (standard)		430
Variance		20
Total direct costs	450	450
Contribution to profit	550	550
Fixed expenses	385	385
Pretax profit	165	165

Commissions, a selling rather than a manufacturing expense, are included in the variable category but are not charged to inventory. This item of cost therefore is not included in the cost flow through work in process and finished goods.

Fixed or period expenses include such items as depreciation, real estate taxes, supervisory salaries, fire insurance, fixed selling expenses, and officers' salaries.

Contribution to profit, also known as marginal income, P/V ratio, and profit-volume relationship, represents the amount of sales dollars left after direct costs. This is a key figure in the determination of the breakeven point—an advantage of the direct costing statement format. This calculation is demonstrated as follows.

Take the $1000 in sales volume as the starting point. If variable costs are 45% of sales ($450 divided by $1000), then 55% of the sales are left to cover fixed costs.

The breakeven point is determined by dividing the fixed costs by the marginal income percentage (percentage of sales dollars left after variable costs are provided for). The computation (385 divided by 55%) gives us a breakeven point of $700. This can be verified as follows.

Breakeven sales volume	$700
Variable costs (45%)	315
Marginal income	385
Fixed costs	385
Pretax profit	0

Since the first computation based on sales of $1000 showed a profit of $165 and the second at breakeven showed no profit, then the entire profit is made in the sales of $300 remaining after breakeven volume is passed. We can verify this as follows.

Sales volume above breakeven	$300
Variable costs (45%)	135
Marginal income	165
Fixed costs	0
Pretax profit	165

We can see from the above that after variable costs of 45% are subtracted from the $300 sales we have a marginal income of $165. Since marginal income is the income after variable costs are provided for, this is the amount left to cover fixed costs and profits. Inasmuch as fixed costs of $385 were already recovered in breakeven sales of $700, the entire amount of $165 is a profit. In conventional usage this profit would have been stated as 16.5% of sales of $1000. Actually, it would be more correct to state the profit as 55% of the sales volume above breakeven. This points up the dynamic nature of the break-even point.

How Cost Flow Differs for Direct Costing

The basic difference between absorption and direct costing is that fixed costs under the latter are not inventoried. Fixed costs therefore bypass the work-in-process and finished goods accounts, going directly to cost of sales. The variable manufacturing costs flow through the accounts in the same manner as in absorption costing procedures. Under standard direct costing the flow utilizes the variance account which is closed out and transferred to the cost of sales account.

The next chapter considers the pros and cons of absorption and direct costing at greater length. However, before leaving the subject of cost flow and valuation of inventories, we should consider the effect on gross profit of the two basic methods of valuing inventories, first-in-first-out (FIFO) and last-in-first-out (LIFO).

Inventory Valuation and Effect on Profits

The inventory value used as the basis for costing sales can result in illusory profits when the method of costing is out of "sync" with current economic conditions. The degree to which profits are illusory varies with the degree of change in the economy (as well as fluctuations in the size of the inventory).

This is demonstrated with an example based on the production and shipment data in Table 14-6.

Table 14-6   Basic Data

	Production (units)	Shipment (units)
Month A	100	0
Month B	100	75
Month C	100	75
Month D	0	75
	300	225
		75 (in inventory)
		300 (produced)

Costing Sales under the FIFO Method

Assume further that unit production costs were $53 in month A, $55 in month B, and $58 in month C, and that the company uses the FIFO method of valuing inventories. The resulting unit production, shipment and inventory costs are shown in Table 14-7.

Table 14-7   FIFO Costing

	Production	Shipments	
Month A	100 units @$53 = $ 5,300	None	
Month B	100 units @$55 = $ 5,500	75 units @$53	= $ 3,975
Month C	100 units @$58 = $ 5,800	25 units @$53, 50 units @$55 = $ 4,075	
Month D	None	50 units @$55, 25 units @$58 = $ 4,200	
			$12,250
		Inventory	
		75 units @$58	4,350
	$16,600		$16,600

An operating statement based on the four months shown in Table 14-7 reflects the following.

Sales (225 units at $60)	$13,500
Cost of sales	12,250
Gross profit	$ 1,250

Since the unit costs are rising—and our assumption is that the rise is due to economic conditions—the use of FIFO costs the units that are sold at lower prices than the units remaining in inventory. In short, part of the increased cost is being deferred in inventory.

Costing Sales under the LIFO Method

Using the same basic data, let us now use LIFO as the method of costing sales and compare the gross profit under the two methods of costing (Table 14-8).

Table 14-8   LIFO Costing

	Production	Shipments	
Month A	100 units @$53 = $ 5,300	None	
Month B	100 units @$55 = $ 5,500	75 units @$55	= $ 4,125
Month C	100 units @$58 = $ 5,800	75 units @$58	= $ 4,350
Month D	None	25 @$58, 25@$55, 25 @$53	= $ 4,150
			$12,625
		Inventory	
		75 units @ $53	3,975
	$16,600		$16,600

The resulting operating statement based on the above follows.

Sales (225 units at $60)	$13,500
Cost of sales	12,625
Gross profit	$ 875

The result on gross profits of the two methods of valuing inventories is recapped as follows.

	FIFO	LIFO
Sales	$13,500	$13,500
Cost of sales	12,250	12,625
Gross profit	$ 1,250	$ 875

It becomes obvious that the results reflected on an operating statement can vary depending on the method used for valuing inventories. Variations in method of treatment of other factors—depreciation, for example—can also affect the reported profits. It is not the intent to delve further into the various factors that can have an effect on the operating statements but rather to point up one of the reasons why it is necessary to go behind the figures that appear on the statement.

PROFITABILITY BY CLASS OF SALES

A total or overall operating statement can represent an average of the profitability of several classes of sales, each with widely divergent results. To continue looking at the overall can deprive management of information that could be valuable in making decisions which would improve profitability.

Some companies, in determining profitability by the various classes, allocate major "below-the-line" expenses such as sales and general and administrative on the basis of the sales volume. This can be just as misleading as using the overall figure for decision making. Consider the following example.

Company A sells its products to several sister divisions as well as to distributors and to other companies. The sales department effort required to sell to sister divisions and to distributors is minimal as compared with the direct contact required in selling to other companies. The major effort in selling to a company's own divisions is in the order entry and billing activity. The same is true when selling to distributors because orders are larger and more routine in nature. But in the sales effort required in selling other companies, the average sale is much smaller; personal contact and extensive travel on the part of the salesman is required.

Under these circumstances, the logical question is: How can you allocate on a pure dollar volume basis?

One will find, in analyzing direct sales, that many companies have a small number of large house accounts. Such accounts are based on the personal contact of one of the executives of the company—rather than a member of the sales staff. Orders from such accounts are often automatic and do not require salesman servicing. Here again, the sales department cost cannot arbitrarily be assigned on the dollar volume basis, otherwise management would be mislead on the profitability of various classes of sales.

Warehousing expenses, likewise, influence product profitability, depending upon the method of assignment of this cost to class of sale. The shelf item type of product generally requires substantial warehousing throughout the country or territory. The customized version of the same product, which is made to order, requires no warehousing. To assign this cost on the basis of sales volume could misstate profitability.

The same principle applies to institutional advertising—the company does not need to advertise in order to sell to one of its divisions. Bad debt expense, likewise, is not incurred by a sister division or by the large, triple A credit-rated house account.

The operating statement shown in Exhibit 14-1 demonstrates how the profitability by class of sales can vary. Note that the total profit amounts to 4.9% of sales of $15,377,000. But when these sales are broken down by sales to other divisions, sales to distributors, and sales made by the company's own sales force through direct selling, the profit varies from 14% for interdivision sales to breakeven for

Exhibit 14-1   Operating Statement by Major Class of Sale

	Total	Inter-division	Distrib-utors	Direct Selling
Gross sales	$15,377,000	$5,126,000	$5,126,000	$5,125,000
Less discounts and allowances	676,000	163,000	513,000	
Royalties	176,000	59,000	59,000	58,000
Net sales	$14,525,000	$4,904,000	$4,554,000	$5,067,000
Cost of sales	11,610,000	3,870,000	3,870,000	3,870,000
Gross operating profit	2,915,000	1,034,000	684,000	1,197,000
Selling expenses	676,000	101,400	101,400	473,200
Product service expenses	220,000	110,000		110,000
Warehouse expenses	144,000	24,000	24,000	96,000
Advertising	801,000		400,500	400,500
Bad-debts	74,000		37,000	37,000
Engineering and product design	242,000	81,000	81,000	80,000
Total expense	$ 2,157,000	$ 316,400	$ 643,900	$1,196,700
Pretax profit	758,000	717,600	40,100	300
Percent Profit on sales	4.9	14.0	0.8	—

direct selling. Interdivision sales are more profitable than the other classes because no advertising expenses are required for this type of selling. At the same time, sales department expenses are minimal. Direct selling, however, requires a high degree of sales effort as well as advertising.

Even the direct sales can be broken down by classes with varying degrees of profitability. Exhibit 14-2 demonstrates how the total

Exhibit 14-2   Breakdown of Direct Selling

	Total Direct Selling	One Large Customer, House Account	Special Custom Line	All Others
Gross Sales	$5,125,000	$1,708,300	$1,708,300	$1,708,400
Less: Discounts and allowances				
Royalties	58,000	19,300	19,300	19,400
Net sales	5,067,000	1,689,000	1,689,000	1,689,000
Cost of sales	3,870,000	1,290,000	1,290,000	1,290,000
Gross operating profit	1,197,000	399,000	399,000	399,000
Selling expenses	473,200	71,000	201,100	201,100
Product service expenses	110,000	36,700	36,700	36,600
Warehouse expenses	96,000	48,000	—	48,000
Advertising	400,500	133,500	133,500	133,500
Bad debts	37,000		18,500	18,500
Engineering and product design	80,000	26,700	26,700	26,600
Total expense	$1,196,700	$ 315,900	$ 416,500	$ 464,300
Pretax profit	300	83,100	(17,500)	(65,300)
Percent profit on sales	—	4.9	(1.0)	(3.8)

direct selling is broken down by three categories: one large customer (house account), special custom line, and all others.

Although the total direct sales category shows breakeven results, the large house account shows a 4.9% profit on sales. This class of sale requires less sales effort because of a standing relationship with one of the nonsales executives. Orders are forwarded regularly on a release basis with no need for salesmen to call on a regular basis. Of the remaining two classes, the special custom line, is less unprofitable because warehousing costs are generally unnecessary for custom products.

Although the percent of profit on sales has been compared for the various classes of sales for illustrative purposes, it is well to bear in mind that the percent of return on investment would be a more appropriate measure of profitability.

SUMMING UP

The operating statement is an important management tool, but unless used wisely it can have its limitations. The professional manager must be familiar with the makeup of the data behind the figures shown in the statement. While the statement shows the cost of sales—representing the manufacturing cost of the products sold— his point of control is not at the cost of sales (output) level but at the input level.

The relationship of manufacturing costs at the input level to the cost of sales level has an effect on inventory and therefore on the size of the investment used as a base for measuring the return on investment.

Of equal importance is the knowledge of profitability of various classes of sales. Just knowing product profitability is not enough because the same product can be sold through various channels with different types of expenses being incurred because of such costs as warehousing, advertising, and field service.

The professional manager, similar to the astronomer and the astronaut, must take a closer look at the details that make up the big picture.

CHAPTER 15

WHICH STATEMENT FORMAT SHALL I LOOK AT?

A proliferation of statement formats can be confusing and aggravating to the busy executive who must have facts on which to base decisions. This chapter discusses four basic formats and demonstrates the use and application of each.

Professional managers are often confused and annoyed by the apparent duplication of financial data received by them in a variety of formats.

The income statement (called operating statement by some and profit and loss statement by others), is perhaps a greater target for such criticism than any other single management report.

Promoters of the total systems concept frequently attempt to reduce the number of such reports. But because many of these groups are not fully conversant with the use and intended purpose of some of the reports, their attempts to eliminate duplication through consolidation are often unsuccessful.

The purpose of this chapter is to discuss the use made of the various statement formats. Knowing this, and knowing a company's specific needs, it is possible to take an approach in the total systems concept that will be more readily accepted.

The reports discussed are those falling into the following general areas:

- Stockholder reporting (Exhibit 15–1)
- Financial accounting (Exhibit 15–2)

- Cost accounting (Exhibit 15–3)
- Budgeting (Exhibit 15–4)

While each of the above requires inclusion of some data common to the others, the essential difference is in the underlying detail contained in the various report formats.

EXHIBIT 15-1: STOCKHOLDER REPORTING

A public accountant, in his role as auditor and "attestor" to the correctness of the data, must review and test the many source figures capsulized in Exhibit 15–1.

Responsibility of the Public Accountant

The public accountant has a responsibility to the stockholders to assure them that the financial data contained in the company's annual report are correct. He has a further responsibility to report the same basic data (but in greater detail) to the Securities Exchange Commission.

d The upper half of Exhibit 15–1 is actually a one-line summary of each of the major classes of income or expense. Note, for example, that net sales are reported without attempting to show the amount of the discounts and other allowances given to customers.

Likewise, cost of products and services sold and operating expenses are shown as single line items without details of their makeup. Depreciation, although already included in the costs and expenses section, is shown on a memo basis for convenience in calculating the cash flow.

In presenting the annual report, some companies compare the current year with the previous one. Some make a five-year comparison, while others will show ten years of history.

Analytical Data

Many annual reports provide statistical data of the type shown in the lower half of Exhibit 15–1. There is very little standardization

Exhibit 15-1 Stockholder Reporting

	Year 6	Year 5	Year 4	Year 3	Year 2	Year 1
Income						
Net sales	$1,279,028	$1,185,231	$943,269	$784,619	$892,516	$742,803
Miscellaneous	16,750	15,220	18,650	14,200	12,600	10,950
	$1,295,778	$1,200,451	$961,919	$798,819	$905,116	$753,753
Costs and expenses						
Cost of products and services sold	$ 895,320	$ 805,957	$613,125	$486,464	$580,135	$519,962
Operating expenses	352,548	321,604	300,562	247,605	268,921	201,045
Other deductions	8,267	1,421	2,032	16,205	1,141	832
Federal income taxes	15,000	32,000	18,500	17,500	24,000	11,000
	$1,271,135	$1,160,982	$934,219	$767,774	$874,197	$732,839
Net income	$ 24,643	$ 39,469	$ 27,700	$ 31,045	$ 30,919	$ 20,914
Provision for depreciation included in costs and expenses	$ 62,345	$ 61,914	$ 50,243	$ 58,619	$ 47,841	$ 51,203
Trend ratio (Year 1 = 100)						
Sales	172%	160%	127%	106%	120%	100%
Cost of sales	172	155	118	94	112	100
Operating expenses	175	160	149	123	134	100
Net income	119	189	132	148	148	100

Exhibit 15-1 (Continued)

	Year 1	Year 2	Year 3	Year 4	Year 5	Year 6
Company						
Sales ratio (sales = 100)						
Net sales	100%	100%	100%	100%	100%	100%
Cost of sales	70	65	62	65	68	70
Gross margin	30%	35%	38%	35%	32%	30%
Operating expenses	27	30	31	32	27	27
Operating margin	3%	5%	7%	3%	5%	3%
Industry						
Sales ratio						
Net sales	100%	100%	100%	100%	100%	100%
Cost of sales	65	62	60	62	65	68
Gross margin	35%	38%	40%	38%	35%	32%
Operating expenses	27	28	27	25	24	22
Operating margin	8%	10%	13%	13%	11%	10%
Trend ratio (Year 1 = 100)						
Industry sales	100%	121%	136%	152%	171%	203%

among the companies whose financial departments include this type of data in their annual reports or in other statements. Usually the more favorable comparisons are highlighted for public consumption.

The illustration shown in Exhibit 15–1 demonstrates several types of analyses that can be used. They are:

- Trend ratios
- Ratio of company costs and expenses to company sales
- Ratio of industry costs and expenses to industry sales

Trend Ratios

This statistical method develops year-to-year percentages for each line item by selecting a base year as 100% and dividing the item in each year by its counterpart in the base year. The illustration in Exhibit 15–1 indicates that operating expenses in Year 6 increased at a greater rate than sales. Sales, for example, are 172% of the base year, while operating expenses are 175%.

Ratio of Company Costs and Expenses to Company Sales

In this type of ratio, the sales in each year become 100%, and each line item in that year is divided by the sales. Note how quickly it can be determined that the operating margin was greatest in Year 3.

Ratio of Industry Cost and Expenses to Industry Sales

These ratios are compiled in the same manner as above, except that they represent industry data. Note how easily one can compare the profit trend for the company with that of the industry. While the company's profit in Year 3 was the best, and Year 4 one of the poorer years (3% profit), Year 4 was a good year for the industry. This comparison shows that for all years the industry generally did better than the company.

A trend ratio for sales in the industry is also shown. A comparison of this figure with the sales trend ratio for the company indicates that the company is not keeping pace with the industry.

EXHIBIT 15-2: FINANCIAL ACCOUNTING

The financial accountant takes the capsulized figures presented in the annual report and "explodes" them into greater detail. He shows, for example, how gross sales have been reduced by returns and allowances. He shows the factory costs that were incurred during the month and the effect of production and shipments on the ending inventory. Expenses are broken down to show how much of this type of expense was incurred in selling, administration, and research and development.

Since factory cost (cost of goods sold) is a major item in this type of company, a further analysis has been made to show the cost flow by the three major elements of cost—material, direct labor, and overhead.

This type of analysis shows, by element of cost, what has happened to the inventory. Total inventories, for example, have increased from $179,064 to $227,660. While all three elements of cost in inventory have increased, the material content in the ending inventory has been reduced from 57 to 52% while labor and overhead content have increased.

This provides a reconciliation of costs incurred during the month with the cost of products sold—the difference being reflected as an inventory change.

EXHIBIT 15-3: COST ACCOUNTING

The cost accountant, in providing his management with more actionable information, normally uses standard costs for valuing production and inventories. Deviations of actual costs from standard are reported as variations or variances.

Measuring Variances—Degrees of Sophistication

Variances can be broken down in different ways. The simplest is to compare total standard costs with total actual costs. While this ap-

Exhibit 15-2 Financial Accounting

	Details
Gross sales	$1,354,150
Less returns and allowances	75,122
Net sales	1,279,028
Cost of products and services sold:	
Beginning inventories	179,064
Purchases, less discounts	506,466
Direct labor	147,931
Manufacturing expenses	289,519
	1,122,980
Less ending inventories	227,660
Cost of sales	895,320
Gross margin (actual)	383,708
Expenses	
Selling and shipping	191,854
Administrative	76,742
Corporate	25,581
Research and development	58,371
Expenses	352,548
Operating margin	31,160
Other income	
Interest	10,235
Royalties	1,515
Rents	5,000
Other income	16,750
Other deductions	
Interest	1,545
Loss on disposal of equipment	5,290
Sundry	1,432
Other deductions	8,267
Income before income taxes	39,643
Federal income taxes	15,000
Net income	24,643

Exhibit 15-2 (Continued)

	Material	Labor	Overhead	Total
	Analysis of Cost of Sales			
Beginning inventories	$102,067	$ 25,069	$ 51,928	$ 179,064
	57%	14%	29%	100%
Purchases	506,466			506,466
Direct labor		147,931		147,931
Overhead			289,519	289,519
	$608,533	$173,000	$341,447	$1,122,980
Ending inventories	116,107	38,702	72,851	227,660
	52%	16%	32%	100%
Total	$492,426	$134,298	$268,596	$ 895,320
Percent of cost	55	15	30	100
Percent of net sales	39	10	21	70

proach has some value in measuring how much excess cost has been incurred in total for the period, more detail is required for effective action to be taken.

The next level of detail might be to identify variations by element of cost, that is, material, direct labor, and overhead. This approach is better than merely showing the total amount of excess cost because it narrows the variance down to specific areas of cost which can be investigated.

A more useful approach is to break down each of the three elements of cost into their major variances as has been demonstrated in Exhibit 15–3.

Managing by Exception

In Exhibit 15–3 the largest unfavorable variance is material substitution, $8165. This indicates that more expensive material was used than called for in the bill of materials. Supplementing this type of information on the exhibit should be a narrative explanation as to where, specifically, the more expensive material was used. Also included in this explanation should be some indication as to why the more expensive material was used and whether this condition has been corrected. The same procedure is followed for all other variances

Exhibit 15-3 Cost Accounting

	Total	Product Line A	Product Line B	Product Line C	Service
Gross sales	$1,354,150	$710,571	$195,770	$319,906	$127,903
Less returns and allowances	75,122	71,057	3,915	150	0
Net sales	$1,279,028	$639,514	$191,855	$319,756	$127,903
Cost of products and services sold					
Standard	843,372	382,586	142,884	292,321	25,581
Standard gross margin	$435,656	$256,928	$ 48,971	$ 27,435	$102,322
Variation					
Material					
Price, Steel	$ 3,176	$ 3,026	$ 150		
Price, Other	8,031	816	7,215		
Usage	5,698	2,614	3,084		
Substitution	8,165	8,129	36		
Sale of scrap material	(5,025)	(3,507)	(1,518)		
Labor					
Rate	2,020	1,810	210		
Efficiency	4,115	3,800	315		
Overhead	25,768	16,410	1,108	$ 8,250	
Total variations	$ 51,948	$ 33,098	$ 10,600	$ 8,250	
Cost of products sold	$ 895,320	$415,684	$153,484	$300,571	$ 25,581
Actual gross margin	$ 383,708	$223,830	$ 38,371	$ 19,185	$102,322
Expenses					
Selling and shipping	$ 191,854				
Administrative	76,742				
Corporate	$ 25,581				
Research and development	58,371				
Expenses	$ 352,548				
Operating margin (loss)	$ 31,160				

—the depth of detail depending upon the relative magnitude of the variance.

This type of report format, as can be seen, further expands upon the information furnished by the financial accountant.

Breakdown of Costs and Variances by Product Line

It is not the intent of a true standard cost system to identify variances by product line, but rather by type of material and by cost center (as well as purchase price variance on material and rate variance on labor).

The cost center, after all, is the point of control. If a product line, by its nature, is more difficult to make, then this is taken into account in establishing the standard cost.

There are instances, however, when it is feasible to identify variances by product line. In such instances an analysis similar to that shown in Exhibit 15–3 can be made. Product line A uses steel, while product line B contains little steel but a fair amount of purchased components. Product line C does not utilize standard costs as yet. Costs of products and services sold for product line C is really actual cost rather than standard. Services too, are shown at actual cost with no variances indicated.

A breakdown of variances by product line, as shown in Exhibit 15-3, indicates to management how much work is required in product lines A and B to achieve the standard gross Margin. The effect of volume on product line C is also shown.

While the product line profitability is carried down only to the actual gross margin level, it is possible that certain of the "below-the-line" expenses can be specifically identified by product line. Exhibit 15-3 could be expanded to reflect this.

EXHIBIT 15-4: BUDGETING

While the budget director uses the same basic format as that used by the financial accountant, he is interested in comparing each of these items with a budget.

Exhibit 15-4 shows how such a comparison is made—a third column indicating the amount by which actuals are over or under the budget. Variations from the budget shown for material, labor, and overhead (manufacturing expenses) in this exhibit are not likely to tie in with those shown in Exhibit 15-3. The reason is that many companies using the financial budgeting approach prepare such budgets annually for the year, with periodic revisions.

Standard costs, however, are based on predetermined standards that are usually frozen for the year and are applied on the basis of the actual level of production. Such standards are more precise because they are intended to measure the performance of a factory.

Exhibit 15-4 Budgeting

	Actual	Budget	Under (Over)
Gross sales	$1,354,150	$1,281,510	($72,640)
Less returns and allowances	75,122	25,276	(49,846)
Net sales	$1,279,028	$1,256,234	($22,794)
Cost of products and services sold			
Beginning inventories	$ 179,064	$ 179,064	
Purchases less discounts	506,466	485,239	($21,227)
Direct labor	147,931	130,456	(17,475)
Manufacturing expenses	289,519	250,978	(38,541)
	$1,122,980	$1,045,737	($77,243)
Less ending inventories	227,660	200,176	(27,484)
Cost of products sold	$ 895,320	$ 845,561	($49,759)
Actual gross margin	$ 383,708	$ 410,673	$26,965
Expenses			
Selling and shipping	$ 191,854	$ 175,250	($16,604)
Administrative	76,742	70,276	(6,466)
Corporate	25,581	25,600	19
Research and development	58,371	50,000	(8,371)
Expenses	$ 352,548	$ 321,126	($31,422)
Operating margin	$ 31,160	$ 89,547	$58,387
Other income			
Interest	$ 10,235	$ 10,000	($ 235)
Royalties	1,515		(1,515)
Rents	5,000	5,000	
Other income	$ 16,750	$ 15,000	($ 1,750)
Other deductions			
Interest	$ 1,545		($ 1,545)
Loss on disposal of equipment	5,290	$ 10,000	4,710
Sundry	1,432		(1,432)
Other deductions	$ 8,267	$ 10,000	$ 1,733
Income before income taxes	$ 39,643	$ 94,547	$54,904
Federal income taxes	15,000	42,000	27,000
Net income	$ 24,643	$ 52,547	$27,904

Overall budgets, however, are intended to provide management with an overview of how the company is performing according to broader parameters established for the year. Each type of report format discussed has a specific purpose and application. The application that is suitable for one company may not be entirely suitable for another. While the basic format and purpose are somewhat standard, they should not be accepted and applied blindly. A report should be tailored to fit the specific needs of the company.

CHAPTER 16

EXPLAINING DEVIATIONS FROM PLANNED PROFITS

The analysis of variances in some companies has become a fine art in the practice of mathematics without really throwing much light on the problem. When the approach is formula-oriented, the amount and type of variance can vary depending upon which formula is used.

When a profit plan is established, the measurement of performance of each of the elements against the plan can be accomplished through the following steps:

1. Comparison of the actual with the plan and determination of the amount of deviation or variance.
2. Analysis of the variance; why did it occur?

By reviewing the variances according to their magnitude, management can single out the major ones for immediate corrective action, leaving the smaller ones to be taken care of as time allows. This is known as management by exception.

While there is little disagreement regarding the importance of explaining the reasons for variance, there is some question as to whether or not an attempt to measure precisely the impact of variations from planned goals is a productive exercise. Corporate structures that include a staff of financial analysts frequently attempt to make such mathematically determined measurements and hold operating heads accountable to conclusions drawn by the staff group. This group is often more interested in justifying its own mathematically derived conclusions than in understanding the true operational problems.

The Planning Executives Institute, recognizing that such measurements are subject to much controversy, even among analysts, invited several of its members who are recognized experts to submit solutions to a set of basic figures.

These figures are included in the problem that follows.

THE PROBLEM

Only by the analysis of profit trends in terms of the four factors (cost, price, volume, mixture) can management take intelligent action by isolating the causes and concentrating action on the *significant* areas that affect profit. The well-known usual calculation is:

change in sales × base profit ratio = due to volume
Actual Sales × change in profit ratio = due to profit ratio

While profit losses or gains due to profit margin ratio originally indicate unfavorable or favorable trends in the *relationships* of sales price and cost, if neither has materially changed from the base period, then a change in mixture is also indicated. Therefore, this general formula is often not sufficient.

But, what *is* volume? And, what *is* mixture? The correct definition of these two seems to raise the hackles of budget and cost men everywhere, for the purpose of analysis is to determine the significance of each factor and avoid glib generalizations.

Is volume "dollar volume"? Or, is it *quantity?* And, is quantity the same thing as *unit volume?* If volume is dollar volume, do we then remove *price* differences first? When we talk of volume (or price, or cost) are we speaking from an overall point of view, that is, *total* sales and profit; or of the individual and several products or product lines which, as individual components, make up the total? Can "mixture" be properly applied to an individual product line within the group? Is the base period a standard?

Because the answers to such questions often lead to the complete confusion of volume and mixture, these questions themselves are not mere fanciful exercises in semantics. For example, in practice, the term mixture is often loosely used to explain *any* profit change which could be due to the normal interplay of variables affecting revenue and cost, that is, quantity and price. Correctly, we believe it explains only the changes in gross profit (and gross profit ratios) that result from the almost inevitable change in the *combination* (or "variety") of products sold when actual results (or forecast results) are compared to the budget or base period. Much of the profit change sometimes attributed to mixture can be due to price, or cost, and/or volume. A change in mixture is a *shift* in the proportions or "weight" of the various products (or product lines) making up the total.

Let us assume some basic and oversimplified data, and then work out the solutions.

THE DATA

Three solutions follow, along with the author's critique.

Base Period

Product	Units	Price Per Unit, ($)	Sales, ($)	Cost Per Unit, ($)	Cost of Sales, ($)	Gross Profit, ($)	Gross Profit Ratio
A	1,000	2.00	2,000	1.25	1,250	750	37.5
B	2,000	3.00	6,000	2.00	4,000	2,000	33.3
C	3,000	1.00	3,000	0.75	2,250	750	25.0
Total	6,000	1.833	11,000	1.25	7,500	3,500	31.8

Comparison Period

Product	Units	Price Per Unit, ($)	Sales, ($)	Cost Per Unit, ($)	Cost of Sales, ($)	Gross Profit, ($)	Gross Profit Ratio
A	2500	2.50	6250	2.00	5000	1250	20.0
B	1000	3.00	3000	1.75	1750	1250	41.66
C	500	0.50	250	0.50	250		
Total	4000	2.375	9500	1.75	7000	2500	26.3

Change from Base Period Plus or (Minus)

Product	Units	Price Per Unit, ($)	Sales, ($)	Cost Per Unit, ($)	Cost of Sales, ($)	Gross Profit, ($)	Gross Profit Ratio
A	+1500	+0.50	+4250	+0.75	+3750	+500	(17.5)
B	(1000)		(3000)	(0.25)	(2250)	(750)	+8.33
C	(2500)	(0.50)	(2750)	(0.25)	(2000)	(750)	(25.0)
Total	(2000)	+0.542	(1500)	+0.50	(500)	(1000)	(5.5)

FIRST SOLUTION

The first step is to agree upon definitions and terms. Intentionally are omitted two terms in the content. Dollar volume—because it is the result of two of the terms—volume and price. Profit ratio—because it is the result of two terms, price and cost, shown independently. Terms are definitions used in the analyses are:

1. Volume—total unit quantity sold.
2. Price—price per unit sold.
3. Cost—cost per unit to manufacture.
4. Mixture—proportions or weight of various products making up the total volume.

To analyze profit, we first look to the basic element that caused that profit or change thereof. That basic element is the unit sold. The first logical step is to determine the degree of change in units sold due to volume, and the degree of change due to mixture. This we can do as follows.

1. To solve for the change in units sold that was due solely to volume, we note, by definition, that the volume declined from 6000 to 4000, in units. If there had been only a change in volume with *no* change in mixture, the sales would have been as indicated in column B.

Product	A Base Period	B Comparison Period	C Change Due to Volume
A	1000	667	−333
B	2000	1333	−667
C	3000	2000	−1000
Total	6000	4000	−2000

Compare from the base period to the comparison period and note that we have accounted for the decline in volume of 2000 units.

2. To solve for the change in units sold due solely to mixture, by definition, we compare the proportions (or weight) of each product to the total as follows.

Product	Base Period Units	Base Period Proportion	Comparison Period Units	Comparison Period Proportion	Change in Proportion
A	1000	16.667%	2500	62.500%	+45.833
B	2000	33.333%	1000	25.000%	− 8.333
C	3000	50.000%	500	12.500%	−37.500
Total	6000	100.000%	4000	100.000%	0

We then multiply the change in proportion (mixture) by the comparison period total to determine the change in units sold due solely to mixture.

Product	Change in Proportion		Comparison Period Total	Change due to Mixture
A	+45.833	×	4000 units	+1.833
B	− 8.333	×	4000 units	− 333
C	−37.500	×	4000 units	−1.500
Total	0			0

Proof of the analysis of units sold:

Product	Base Period	Comparison Period	Total Change	Analysis of Due to Volume	Change Due to Mixture
A	1000	2500	+1500	− 333	+1.833
B	2000	1000	−1000	− 667	− 333
C	3000	500	−2500	−1000	−1.500
Total	6000	4000	−2000	−2000	0

Having determined the degree of change in units sold due to volume and mixture, analysis of gross profit change becomes simplified:

1. Change in gross profit due to volume:

Product	Base Period Gross Profit per Unit ($)		Change in Units Sold Due to Volume		Change in Gross Profit Due to Volume ($)
A	0.75	$\times$	$-$ 333	$=$	$-$ 250
B	1.00	$\times$	$-$ 667	$=$	$-$ 667
C	0.25	$\times$	-1000	$=$	$-$ 250
Total			-2000		-1167

2. Change in gross profit due to mixture:

Product	Base Period Gross Profit per Unit ($)		Change in Units Sold Due to Mixture		Change in Gross Profit due to Mixture ($)
A	0.75	$\times$	$+1.833$	$=$	$+1375$
B	1.00	$\times$	$-$ 333	$=$	$-$ 333
C	0.25	$\times$	-1.500	$=$	$-$ 375
			0		$+$ 667

3. Change in gross profit due to price:

Product	Change in Price Unit		Units Sold Comparison Period		Change in Gross Profit Due to Price ($)
A	$+0.50$	$\times$	2500	$=$	$+1250$
B	0	$\times$	1000	$=$	0
C	-0.50	$\times$	500	$=$	$-$ 250
Total			4000		$+1000$

4. Change in gross profit due to cost:

Product	Change in Cost per Unit [a]	Units Sold Comparison Period	Change in Gross Profit Due to Cost ($)
A	-0.75	2500	-1875
B	$+0.25$	1000	$+$ 250
C	$+0.50$	500	$+$ 125
Total		4000	-1500

[a]Effect on gross profit.

Summary

Product	Due to Volume($)	Due to Price($)	Due to Cost($)	Due to Mixture($)	Total Change($)
A	− 250	+1250	−1875	+1375	+ 500
B	− 667	0	+ 250	− 333	− 750
C	− 250	− 250	+ 175	− 375	− 750
Total	−1167	+1000	−1500	+ 667	−1000

SECOND SOLUTION

The second solution has been summarized in Exhibit 16–1.

Assumptions

1. Product lines are considered to be individual products. Therefore changes in price per unit or cost per unit are due to specific changes in price or cost of individual products and not caused by mix, which could be the case in a multiproduct product line.

2. Base period is the forecast or budget for a particular month. Comparison period is the actual results for that particular month.

3. Base period cost per unit is the established standard cost (absorption method). The standard cost of each product is the same for both the base period and the comparison period.

Comparison period cost per unit is the actual cost per unit after allocating all production costs for the period to the individual products. It is the standard cost adjusted by volume and expense variances incurred during the comparison period.

Comments on Change in Gross Profit Due to:

Sales Volume

This is the change in unit sales at base period prices.

The difference in sales dollars above due to volume is:

Base period sales	$11,000
Comparison period sales at base period price	8,500
Decrease in sales volume	($ 2,500)

To eliminate the mix factor in the calculation of gross profit change, the change in sales volume is multiplied by the base period gross profit ratio (31.8%) to determine the change in gross profit due to change in sales volume.

Exhibit 16-1 Gross Profit Analysis

Product	Comparison Period Units Sold	Base Period Price Each ($)	Base Period Standard Cost Each ($)	Comparison Period Unit Sales at Base Period Price and Standard Cost Sales ($)	Comparison Period Unit Sales at Base Period Price and Standard Cost Standard Cost ($)	Comparison Period Unit Sales at Base Period Price and Standard Cost Gross Profit Ratio (%)
A	2,500	2.00	1.25	5,000	3,125	37.5
B	1,000	3.00	2.00	3,000	2,000	33.3
C	500	1.00	0.75	500	375	25.0
Total	4,000			8,500	5,500	35.3
Base period sales and cost				11,000	7,500	31.8
Comparison period increase (decrease)				(2,500)	(2,000)	3.5

Change in gross profit due to:

		Increase (decrease)
Sales volume	($2,500) × 31.8% =	(795)
Sales price	$9,500 − $8,500 =	1,000
Sales mix	3.5% × $8,500 =	295
Cost variances from standard	$5,500 − $7,000	(1,500)
Total change in gross profit		(1,000)

Sales Price

This is the difference between the actual comparison period sales ($9500) and the comparison period sales priced at base period prices ($8500).

Sales Mix

By calculating comparison period sales at base period prices ($8500), and comparison period cost at standard (base period) cost ($5500), we can calculate a gross profit ratio (35.3%) which does not give effect to price, cost, or volume changes, when compared to the base period gross profit (31.8%). The only change that affects this change in ratio (3.5%) is the change in the mix of products sold.

Cost Variances

This is the difference between comparison period (actual) costs of sales ($7000) and the standard (base period) cost of actual units sold during the comparison period ($5500). These variances would normally be further analyzed as to cause within the framework of the standard cost system as follows.

1. Direct material use variance
2. Direct material price variance
3. Direct labor variance
4. Burden expense variance
5. Burden volume variance

THIRD SOLUTION

Semantics

Quantity

The number of units of a product. Or, where a number of products are in identical units, the number of units of such group of products. Where the units of product X are different from those of product Y, there can be no single unit applicable to the two products as a group. For instance, the "TBA" line of the oil refineries and marketers: This is tires, batteries, and accessories. Obviously such a product line has no common unit.

Dollar Sales

The dollar value of sales of a product or group of products. This can also be called sales volume or just volume.

Ground rules determine whether dollar sales is before or after such adjustments as cash discounts, freight returns and allowances.

Mix

Mix is the relationship of the quantity of each product to the total quantity of a group of products including the one concerned.

Considering product line A only:

1. Change in gross profit due to quantity:
Comparison period was 2500 units, against 1000 for the base period. On the excess 1500 units, base period gross profit was 37.5%. So change in quantity times base period gross profit ratio

$1500 \times 37.5\%$	=	\$ 1125

2. Change in gross profit due to price per unit:
The price in the comparison period was \$2.50 per unit, against \$2.00 for the base period. So for each of the 2500 units of the comparison period the price was \$0.50 higher. Since this price was not affected by the cost (and did not affect the cost) it appears directly in gross profit.

$\$0.50 \times 2500$	=	1250

3. Change in gross profit due to cost per unit:
In the comparison period cost per unit was \$2.00 against \$1.25 in the base period. So for the quantity of the comparison period, cost per unit was \$0.75 higher. (This is unfavorable to gross profit and therefore negative.)
Change in cost per unit times comparison period quantity

$-\$0.75 \times 2500$	=	-1875
Total		\$ 500

4. Proof: Gross profit on product A:

Comparison period		base period		
\$1250	minus	750	equals	500

Similar calculations are made for products B and C with this result:

Change in gross profit due to	Product A($)	Product B($)	Product C($)	Total
Quantity	1125	−1000	− 625	− 500
Price per unit	1250	0	− 250	1000
Cost per unit	−1875	250	125	−1500
Total change in gross profit	500	− 750	− 750	−1000

The effect of mix is an entirely separate calculation, as follows:

	Product A	Product B	Product C	Total
Base period quantity	1000	2000	3000	6000
Base period mix	17%	33%	50%	100%
Comparison period quantity distributed on the base period mix	680	1320	2000	4000
Comparison period gross profit per unit	$0.50	$1.25	0	
Comparison period adjusted gross profit	$340	$1650	0	$1990
Comparison period actual gross profit				2500
Effect of the change in mix				$ 510

That definition applies where the units of all products in the group are identical. The term mix may also be used, however, for heterogeneous groups.

The relationship of the dollar sales of each product in a group of products to the total dollar sales of the group.

AUTHOR'S CRITIQUE

As is obvious, there are differences in the three solutions even with a rather simple basic problem. Imagine the magnitude of potential differences that would arise in the analysis of business situations far more complex than this simple problem.

Too many analysts resort to the "magic of mathematics" in presenting financial analyses to their managements. The practical business man looks with suspicion on the formula approach to analyzing deviations from profit.

The sales manager points out that his job is to sell the facilities of the factory rather than specific predetermined products in certain predetermined quantities. To point an accusing finger at him because his actual sales incurred a mixture variance which had an unfavorable effect on profit recovery is not always in the best interests of the company. Had he avoided the sales of certain less profitable products in order to minimize the mixture variance, he would have suffered a volume variance because customers buy what they need rather than what the supplier wants to sell them. Also, the practical sales manager points out that the unfavorable volume variance assigned as being his responsibility is frequently caused by the factory not being able to ship the product in time, therefore the customer buys elsewhere.

The manufacturing superintendent in turn, professes that he could not ship the product in time because the sales department did not allow sufficient lead time (usually this is the customer's dictum). He mentions in passing that the cost variance is not correct because the standard product cost is based on standards which assume reasonably long runs. Because of the current short runs and the squeeze for reduced inventories, he cannot be measured by standards that assume reasonable-sized runs—therefore the cost variances are not correctly attributable to him entirely, as is implied by the terminology. All in all, it behooves the analyst to get down to cases and to explain deviations in forecasted profits through a down-to-earth understandable and logical explanation of these factors rather than the mathematics that spill out through application of a textbook formula.

If there were a price decline, or a price increase, he should point out the impact of this change on the *major* items sold that month—but not spend valuable clerical time calculating the effect of a sales price change on every item sold whether its effect was significant or not. He should point out volume variance to his management in such terms as indicating that the fixed costs of $100,000 were not completely absorbed that month because the level of operations was only 80% of normal, therefore $20,000 was unabsorbed. The attempt to isolate mix variance usually proves to be fruitless because of the difficulty of separating it from volume and because of the difficulty in explaining and defining.

In summary, the analyst can perform a far better service by making translations for the operating man into denominators that he understands and with which he deals on an everyday basis. This means that the analyst must separate himself from his desk and computer, and spend more time in those areas and with those people who are closest to the pulse of activity. He must make realistic evaluations on a day-by-day basis and substitute this approach for the month-end mathematics.

CHAPTER 17

ALTERNATIVE COSTING METHODS

Executives who must run their businesses profitably are confused by the diversity of opinion among their professional advisers. Do such executives care whether the cost system is called "direct" or "absorption," or are they primarily interested in results?

A great deal has been written in the past two decades on the virtues of direct costing versus absorption versus distribution costing. Like our two-party system of government, members of the accounting profession have developed "pro" and "con" points of view. Either they enthusiastically endorse the one costing concept or they condemn it. This chapter explores a number of considerations and tries to evaluate the arguments advanced. Since direct and absorption costing proponents raise the loudest arguments we will discuss this.

HISTORY OF DIRECT COSTING AND ABSORPTION COSTING

The deluge of literature on direct costing in recent years fosters the general belief that direct costing is a new concept. Belying this general assumption is the following excerpt which appeared in the February 1906 issue of *System*.

"In estimating the net profit or loss to be expected from choice of action, the first step is to pick out the units of expense (and receipts) suitable for measuring the effects of the particular class of action. Direct expense per unit subtracted from direct receipts per unit gives them direct net revenue per unit, or net contribution per

231

unit towards all those expenses which are outside the sphere of influence of action, and which are with respect to it just as much 'fixed charges' as are those especial charges which are 'fixed', or invariable, with respect to all choices of action alike. This net revenue per unit being multiplied by quantity gives in comparative form the total difference in net profit or loss capable of being caused by choice."

Obviously, direct costing is not new—it predates absorption costing. This is logical because high fixed costs, as we know them today, did not exist in the early years of this century. In fact, in the early 1900s profits were calculated before any provision was made for amortizing equipment costs. As soon as the amount of profit became known, a decision was made as to how much depreciation would be deducted from the current year's profits.

As mechanization increased, investment in equipment grew larger and larger. The use of judgment in determining the amount of depreciation to be taken into expense was considered to be too haphazard—the need for a more scientific approach became obvious. The method adopted was to ascertain the useful life of the asset, determine the annual depreciation provision, and then include the annual cost in an overhead (burden) rate based on an indicator of activity such as direct labor. When the level of activity for the period became known, the overhead rate was extended by the direct labor volume, and this became the cost transfer to inventory. This is how absorption costing was born.

The controversy between advocates of direct costing and absorption costing involves two areas: management reporting and product pricing.

MANAGEMENT REPORTING

In this area the supporters of direct costing are principally interested in the simplicity of reporting afforded by the direct costing concept.

In a direct costing format, direct or variable costs are segregated from fixed or period costs. A profit contribution calculation is made after direct costs are deducted from sales. This profit or marginal contribution can be conveniently compared with period costs to show the impact of volume of sales. The amount of profit must be great enough to cover all fixed or period costs to achieve a breakeven situation.

Early writers and speakers on the subject of direct costing challenged the absorption costing practice of allocating period-type costs to the various product lines. They argued that, since committed costs were there anyway, nothing was to be gained by spreading these costs to products when determining profitability. Their recommendation for an operating statement format by product line is shown in Exhibit 17–1.

Exhibit 17-1   Product Line Operating Statement

	Total	Product A	Product B	Product C
Sales	$1,000,000	$100,000	$410,000	$490,000
Variable costs				
Material	170,000	20,000	60,000	90,000
Direct labor	118,000	8,000	40,000	70,000
Overhead	142,000	12,000	55,000	75,000
Commissions	60,000	6,000	24,000	30,000
Total variable costs	490,000	46,000	179,000	265,000
Variable cost of sales (%)	49	46	44	54
Fixed costs				
Overhead	300,000			
Administration	25,000			
Selling	112,000			
Total fixed costs	437,000			
Profit before taxes	73,000			

Total sales and direct (variable) costs are broken down by products. The total variable cost as a percentage of sales indicates that product B is the most profitable because a greater percentage of the sales dollar is left to cover fixed costs than is left for Products A and C. Product C is the least profitable because the percentage left to cover fixed costs is the smallest of the three.

Critics of direct costing were quick to contest the validity of this method for determining product profitability. They asserted that the investment required to produce various products differed; therefore profitability could not be determined without recognizing these differences. A car rental agency could be used to illustrate this point. Assume that various makes in the low priced compact, the medium, and the luxury sizes are rented. Gauging profitability on an overall basis without considering the differences in depreciation in the Cadillac, Ford, and Volkswagen would be quite misleading. More recent writers and speakers on direct costing have recognized the need to consider fixed costs in determining product profitability.

The argument raised by the direct costers against absorption costing is that when volume is higher than normal a greater amount of fixed costs is absorbed into production and therefore transferred to inventory. The difference between the amount absorbed and the amount which, under direct costing would be considered a period cost, is reflected as a favorable volume variance. Conversely, if the volume of production is lower than normal, a lesser amount of fixed cost would be absorbed into inventory. The difference between this amount and that which would have been reflected as a period expense becomes an unfavorable volume variance. Direct costers argue that many nonaccounting managers are confused by accounting statements that reflect volume variances.

Also, because of the difference in method of treating fixed costs, profits under absorption costing procedures fluctuate with changes in production—profits are greater when production increases, and vice versa. Under direct costing profits fluctuate with sales, rather than with production.

Whether one sides with the direct or absorption costers depends on one's point of view as to what costs should be charged into inventory. Consider the case of a company that automates a hand assembly operation which requires 10 man-hours per unit. At $2 per hour this results in a direct labor cost of $20 per unit. If the machine costs $100,000, has a life of 10 years, and produces 1000 units per year, the cost per unit is $10. In this example depreciation expense has been substituted for direct labor cost. It is rather difficult to build a logical case for inventorying the entire cost of the hand assembly operation but not inventorying the depreciation which amounts to 50% of the original direct labor cost. This would be the case under pure direct costing theory.

Direct costing advocates recognize the pressure from major sources to provide full costs. These are:

1. The Internal Revenue Service and the Securities and Exchange Commission, both of whom require that inventories be valued at full manufacturing cost.

2. Company managers who, pressured by the forces of competition and the relentless demand for higher wages, try to reduce overall costs through the introduction of labor-saving equipment. The operating manager insists on being given information that discloses full product costs so that he can ascertain whether the investment in automation is paying off.

3. Operating executives are continually under pressure to show profitable results. When their operations are highly seasonal, direct costing results in lower profits during inventory accumulation periods. Accordingly, these executives insist that period costs be deferred in inventory.

4. Companies doing business with the government find strong objection to the use of direct costing because of the need to assign period costs to the contract. Government auditors always become suspicious of large pools of expense that are allocated. The suspicion stems from fear that the method of allocation favors the commercial end of the business.

Even when a full absorption standard cost system is in use, auditors are reluctant to accept standards that result in large variances—because of the need to allocate these by some arbitrary method that might favor the commercial products.

Proponents of direct costing, recognizing that these requests must be fulfilled, have proposed that such costs as depreciation and related support services be assigned to the products to which these costs are related without going through the absorption costing process.

This recommended procedure, while suitable for a simple operation in which only a few items are involved, is inadequate for more complex situations. The reason is that such period costs as depreciation and related services must be identified by the cost center or manufacturing process before they can be identified by product. Since the products of most manufacturers are a mixture of parts and sub-assemblies which flow through a number of processes, each represented by different cost centers, overhead can be assigned on an equitable basis only through the absorption process. Then, as the various parts and subassemblies, many of which are common to a number of products, are put together to form a finished product, each product is assigned its full share of overhead cost—both fixed and variable.

Take, for example, the following hypothetical illustration of two radios. Radio A has manual tuning but radio B utilizes push buttons. As a result, radio B requires a greater amount of metal stamping and plastic molding of the parts making up the push button assemblies. This means more plating, painting, and hot stamping at overhead rates which are relatively high because of the greater use of higher cost equipment in these operations. The computation of overhead costs by process for the two products is demonstrated in Exhibit 17-2.

Exhibit 17-2   Comparison of Overhead Costs for Two Radios

| | | Overhead Cost per 100 Radios | | | |
| | Overhead Cost per Hour ($) | Radio A | | Radio B | |
		Hours	Overhead Cost ($)	Hours	Overhead Cost ($)
Metal stamping	10.00	15	150.00	20	200.00
Plating	7.50	5	37.50	7	52.50
Painting	6.75	2	13.50	3	20.25
Plastic molding	8.50	10	85.00	12	102.00
Hot stamping	3.50	2	7.00	3	10.50
Assembly	3.00	66	198.00	68	204.00
		100	491.00	113	589.25
Overhead cost per hour			4.91		5.21

Note that the overhead cost per hour for radio A is $4.91, while the same cost for radio B is $5.21. This cost difference must be recognized in the selling prices of the two radios. The most accurate method for determining this difference is the recognition of cost center overhead rates. This is the essence of absorption costing.

Absorption costers seem to have the weight of government authorities and company managers on their side.

However, absorption costing supporters who blindly reject a report format merely because they disagree with direct costing theory are depriving their managements of a useful analytical tool which is not readily available in the conventional absorption costing format.

PRODUCT PRICING

Supporters of direct costing with respect to product pricing stress the importance of marginal pricing—where direct costs are compared with selling prices of various products to determine the amount of the selling price left (after direct costs) to cover fixed costs and profits. This information is frequently used to "shave" prices by willingness to accept less than full recovery of fixed costs.

The basic assumption is that by reducing prices volume will increase. Although the profit per unit will be smaller, the increased volume will result in a greater total profit. In a check of 14 companies, it was found that almost half stated they used the marginal contribution concept for pricing.

Marginal pricing advocates meet strong resistance from absorption costing proponents who remind them that price reductions are only temporary because competitors react quickly to meet the reduced price—with the result that prices are reduced but the anticipated increase in volume does not materialize. Another disadvantage frequently cited is that the marginal approach to pricing, if not carefully controlled, could result in a "houseful" of unprofitable business.

As companies automate certain products and reduce direct costs, it is conceivable that marginal contribution approaches to pricing could, in addition to these reductions, result in selling prices that further reduce the recovery of fixed costs that permitted the reduction of direct costs in the first place.

Supporters of absorption costing suggest that a more logical method of competitive pricing is to:

1. Spread fixed costs on the basis of optimum utilization of equipment. If purchase of a machine was justified on the basis of

operating two full shifts, then spread the fixed costs over the volume generated by a full two-shift operation. The selling price will then provide for a recovery of investment on a competitive but equitable basis, thereby eliminating guesswork.

2. Base direct labor and material costs included in the selling price on an efficient operation exclusive of excessive rework, scrap, and downtime.

Use of this approach in developing cost-selling price comparisons results in consistency among the various products in a line and these same costs can be used as standards to measure performance.

SUMMING UP

Direct costing provides information to management which is invaluable for profit planning and control. It includes such techniques as breakeven analysis, profit planning, profit-volume relationships, and determination of relative profitability of products in the line.

While some direct costing advocates consider marginal pricing an important tool for management, absorption costing proponents make a good point when they emphasize that a more logical method for costing products is to base costs on optimum utilization of equipment, direct labor, and material. The same cost used for product costing and competitive pricing would provide management with a measuring stick to evaluate performance against these standards.

Although direct costing is based on the concept that fixed costs are charged off as period costs, IRS and SEC requirements for full costing of inventories necessitate a change in approach in this respect. The modification proposed by the direct costers, although probably acceptable to the government agencies, does not equitably assign fixed costs to the various products (where there are significant disparities in amount of investment) without pursuing the absorption costing process through use of cost center overhead rates.

Executives responsible for operating their businesses on a profitable basis in a highly competitive environment are confused by the diversity of opinion among the professionals upon whom they rely for advice. They do not care whether the cost system is called direct costing, absorption costing, or any other name. Nor are they interested in becoming arbiters in an academic debate. But if management were asked to arbitrate, the decision would be: "Utilize the best features of all systems."

CHAPTER 18

SUMMING UP

If the three sections of this book were to be labeled with a single-word description, those three words would be: measurement, efficiency, and feedback. Accordingly, this chapter recaps the indicators used for measurement, stresses the need for efficient operations, and discusses the importance of correcting common defects in providing information to management.

The end purpose of business is to make a profit. In addressing itself to a good profit profile, this book has taken three basic steps which might be restated under the following one-word captions: measurement, efficiency, feedback.

MEASUREMENT

Profits are properly measureable through the indicator commonly referred to as return on investment. Measurement of a company's own results is not sufficient for assuring a good profile—it is important that the results be compared with those of competition. This kind of information is available in annual reports of competitors and in trade association statistics. An illustration of how one company compared itself with its major competitor is demonstrated in Exhibits 18-1 and 18-2. The source of information on the competitor, designated company A, came from published annual reports.

Exhibit 18-1 compares the two companies as to the frequency with which their respective investments are turned over in terms of sales. Company B noted that its competitor, company A, consistently

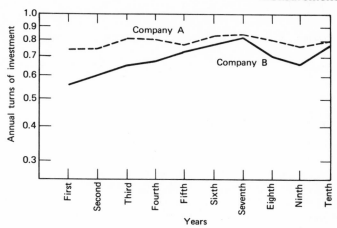

Exhibit 18-1 Annual Turns of Investment—Company A versus Company B*

turned its investment over more frequently over the entire ten-year period studied. To obtain a better insight as to the reason, Exhibit 18-2 was prepared. In this exhibit the capital expenditures for both companies over the same ten-year period were plotted.

In reviewing the total expenditures, it quickly became evident that company B's pattern did not follow its competitor's in two ways:

1. When Company A was expanding from the second through the fifth years, company B went into a period of retrenchment. Company A was therefore able to make inroads by increasing its share of the market for a new product.

2. Company B, in order to protect itself from loss of sales, decided to increase its capital expenditures—which it did between the fifth and seventh years.

Exhibit 18-2 demonstrates that company B was not only slow in moving into an expanding market for its product, but when it did expand it tried to compress into two years the growth that company A took three years to achieve. The result was that the growth was

* Investment defined as stockholder equity plus long-term debt Annual

$$\text{turns} = \frac{\text{Sales}}{\text{Investment as defined above}}$$

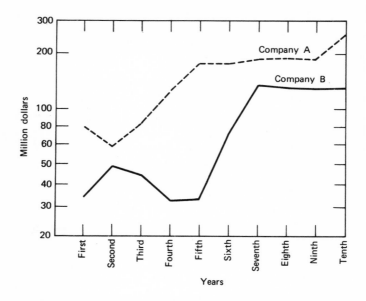

Exhibit 18-2   Capital Expenditures—Company A versus Company B

not efficiently achieved. Although sales rose sharply and brought about improved turnover of investment, profits did not move correspondingly. Return on investment for company B, therefore, did not keep up with company A.

It is not enough to measure the return alone—there are other indicators, such as utilization of equipment and other facilities, that must also be closely monitored.

The foregoing indicators are important because they influence the volume level. Proper volume levels, assuming that they are not attained through arbitrary marginal pricing practices, are the most important single factor in determining a company's profitability profile. They are far more important than the gains that accrue from keeping dollar spending within the budget.

The importance of proper pricing cannot be overemphasized. Companies whose pricing practices are based on the arbitrary marginal pricing approach often find, after a period of time, that the percentage of sales made on this "bargain basement" basis keeps increasing until practically all sales prices have been cut so that recovery of fixed costs has been greatly reduced. In addition, the arbitrary method has resulted in distortions in pricing among models in the same family of products. An economy model, for example, can become more profitable than a deluxe version whose price has been reduced in order to increase volume.

Competitive pricing does not require "giving away" the fixed costs. Fixed costs should be recovered on the basis of operating at practical capacity or optimum volume. Optimum volume is determined in the same manner in which a company decides to invest money in a new machine. If the cost of such a purchase is, say, $240,000, the management satisfies itself that it will be able to obtain sales in sufficient volume to support a two-shift operation for 80% of the available hours. The unit fixed cost of the product at this volume should be the amount recoverable in the selling price, not some amount arbitrarily determined by mathematics of convenience.

While volume indicators are important, one cannot overlook the importance of economic indicators. A company, in monitoring its performance against competitors, must also be attuned to economic trends. By knowing that the economy is rising in a particular sector, a company is given notice that more business is becoming available. Its course of action, then, becomes obvious—gear up to meet the volume.

EFFICIENCY

Though volume is important to a company's profitability profile, the impact of cost effectiveness should not be ignored. Some volume-minded company executives are so intent upon building volume and becoming big that too little attention is paid to other important areas. This can result in high costs and decreased profits.

Cost effectiveness usually addresses itself to the three basic elements of cost: material, direct labor, and overhead.

Material

Companies in which material is the predominant element of cost would do well to look critically at their practices in purchasing, scheduling delivery to the plant, and monitoring inventory obsolescence.

Purchasing often becomes an established routine in which the function of ordering and obtaining quotations is done by rote. This can be remedied by rotating buyers from time to time. It has the effect of introducing new thinking and different approaches. In a well-organized purchasing function, the buyer is continually on the lookout for lower cost substitute materials; he visits the manufacturing facilities of his principal suppliers and he periodically visits the manufacturing facilities of his own company to see how the material is used and what problems are encountered with his purchases in the manufacturing process.

When materials represent a high unit cost, so that storage requires a high investment, progressive buyers arrange for more frequent deliveries directly to production lines. Frequently, such deliveries are made on a daily basis so that storage costs and rehandling are minimized.

Spoilage should be carefully monitored in the early stages of the manufacturing process to detect flaws and to correct them before investment in additional labor and overhead is made.

Direct Labor

When direct labor is a high element of cost, attention should be directed toward possible automation, better balancing of production lines, and the training of operators to avoid spoiled work.

Overhead

When overhead is high because of automated facilities, good tooling, efficient maintenance, and good scheduling of material flow are important. This means that service department personnel, such as production control, purchasing, maintenance, and quality control must work as a coordinated team.

Companies that have been most successful at cost effectiveness are those that concentrate on major cost items and pursue their goals of cost reduction in a consistent and coordinated manner.

FEEDBACK

Feedback is merely another name for two-way communication. When an action is taken by management, feedback procedures must, as in all communication networks, report the results of the action in terms of appropriate and actionable denominators.

To one management group the results of sales effort might be reported in terms of actual sales as compared with planned sales, the differences being expressed in dollar variances from plan. To another management group within the same company, actual and planned sales may best be reported in terms of share of the market. To still another group feedback may be in terms of actual sales by salesmen compared with each of their quotas.

The same principle applies to costs. The general manager in charge of several plants is interested in total sales and net profits as compared with the budget or plan for each of these plants. The individual managers of each plant concentrate on the variances from standard cost—since they frequently have no control of sales.

The foremen within the plants are more interested in such feedback information as scrap reports, labor efficiencies, and equipment utilization within their departments. The feedback is in terms of hourly scrap reports when the product is such that hour-to-hour control is required. In other cases in which an hour-to-hour type of control is not required, scrap reporting can be based on daily reports. Similarly, in labor efficiency feedback, reports can transmit the information to foremen on a daily basis—or less frequently, depending upon the nature of the operation and the unit value of the product.

With the advent of the computer and its ability to process masses of data quickly, many managers have been subjected to an avalanche of reports so detailed that all their working hours could well be devoted merely to studying the contents.

The answer to improved feedback is not in more reports in greater detail; it is in better analysis and meaningful summarization of the data to make them more actionable. A weekly report showing the efficiencies of various operators may be perfectly adequate under normal conditions. However, for a new employee it may be necessary to provide the information on a daily basis so that progress may be closely monitored during the probationary period. Here, the computer should provide a daily report for new employees only. It should show the cumulative labor efficiency from the date of hire and report the efficiency for the current day. This report should be a means for feeding back to the personnel department, as well as the foreman, the effectiveness of the new hire. If the new employee does not meet the job requirements within the prescribed period, he should be terminated or transferred to work for which he is better qualified. At such time as the probation period is over, new employees can be blended into the weekly report and the detail eliminated.

Unfortunately, many data processing centers find it more convenient to standardize on the lowest common denominator of information required rather than make a selective analysis. This is an important reason why the computer has not lived up to expectations in improving feedback. The obvious answer is for management to specify what information it needs to run the company rather than letting the "tail wag the dog."

Misuse of the computer is not the only reason that executives find feedback deficient. Analysts responsible for providing management with the reasons for variances from standard cost are sometimes prone to develop comfortable routines and ivory tower approaches that smack of mathematical exercises rather than probing in depth through direct participation with the operating managers. Use of mathematical formulas for discerning the type of and reason for variance is one of the convenience approaches that deprives the executive of reliable data needed for assuring profitability. While the formula approach is sound in theory, it can be misleading for two reasons:

1. The answer varies depending upon who applies the formula.
2. Use of a formula tends to make the analyst too mechanical.

The answer to this problem is to reject any analytical work performed mechanistically. The analyst, in providing actionable feedback to the executive responsible for profitable operations, must probe deeply and must do his analytical work where the action is. This is the only way that management can be assured of receiving feedback that truly represents two-way communication.

Measurement, efficiency, and feedback can be likened to the three legs of a tripod supporting a business seeking a better profile for profitability. The tripod can be adjusted to any height that may be required for the particular business, but in lengthening the three legs all are of equal importance.

INDEX

249